Cinema Under the Stars

America's Love Affair with the Drive-In Movie Theater

Elizabeth McKeon and Linda Everett

Cumberland House
Nashville, Tennessee

Published by Cumberland House Publishing, Inc., 431 Harding Industrial Drive, Nashville, Tennessee 37211.

Cover design: Harriette Bateman
Cover art: Andy Thomas
Interior design: Mary Sanford

Library of Congress Cataloging-in-Publication Data

McKeon, Elizabeth, 1962–
    Cinema under the stars : America's love affair with the drive-in movie theater / Elizabeth McKeon and Linda Everett.
       p.   cm.
    Includes bibliographical references and index.
    ISBN 1-58182-002-X (pbk. : alk. paper)
    1. Drive-in theaters--United States--History.   I. Everett, Linda,
1946–   .   II. Title.
PN1993.5.U6M315   1998
791.43'0973--dc21   98-44890
                                               CIP

Printed in the United States of America
1 2 3 4 5 6 7—04 03 02 01 00 99 98

To the Smith's Ranch Drive-In theater in Twentynine Palms, California, where I watched '60s Elvis movies from the back of my horse. To the Starlite Drive-In (also in Twentynine Palms), where in 1984 my daughter and I became part of a Purple Rain *party that lasted five nights and became an event.*

—*Linda Everett*

To Richard M. Hollingshead Jr., the inventor of the drive-in movie theater.

—*Elizabeth McKeon*

An elaborate pair of 3-D viewing glasses. *(Terry Lee Roth collection)*

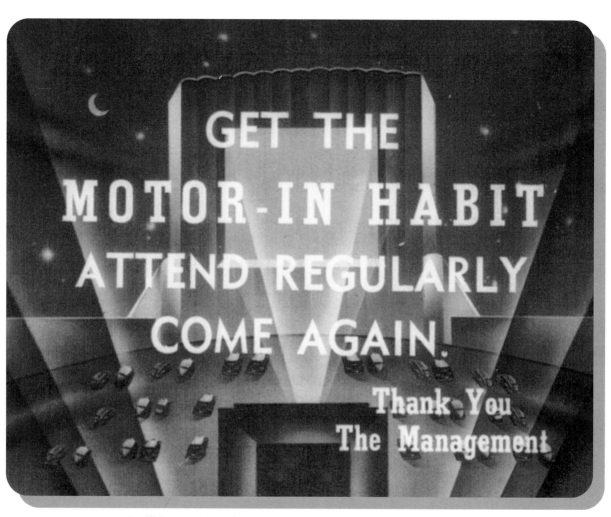

A still from a Filmack promotional trailer. *(Mark Bialek collection)*

Now Playing

The occupants of this vintage car are about to experience the "talkies" in a new way at the Pico-Westwood Drive-In Movie Theater in Los Angeles, California, 1934. *(Bison Archives)*

Foreword

As I look back on my childhood during the early 1960s, I fondly recall the small Maryland town where I lived. Essex was the type of place where every convenience was within walking distance. Lined along the avenue, which ran through the heart of downtown, was an A&P grocery store, Woolworth's, and Reed's drugstore. My favorite haunts included Tubman's toy store and the pet and hobby shop located next door.

While Essex had just about everything, the one thing it didn't have was a movie theater. Unfortunately, the only one in town had burned to the ground. If we kids wanted to see the latest Hollywood release it was up to Dad and Mom to drive us to a theater in another town. And if neither of them could allot a block of time to sit through a matinee of Walt Disney films, we would usually venture into the theater alone.

Indeed, it was often difficult to find a theater featuring movies that catered to the entire family. But I soon discovered the answer to this dilemma—the drive-in movie theater.

I cannot remember when I first experienced the thrill of attending an "ozoner," but since then I have become a seasoned veteran. When you go to a drive-in it isn't important if the movies you have paid to see are memorable or not, it's the pure magic of being there that really counts.

From the sound of rubber tires riding over coarse gravel to the flicker of lights piercing through a misty fog-laden sky, the drive-in theater is a place unlike any indoor theater. At the drive-in, families mingle and interact with one another, friendships are made, children play, and love-smitten couples cuddle under a starlit blanket. To me, the drive-in movie theater is a sanctuary.

One of the most fascinating aspects of the history of the drive-in is all the things that had to be invented: the concession stand, screen towers, ticket booths, speakers, and speaker poles. The layout of an indoor theater had to be converted into a system that replaced regular theater seats with automobiles.

Of all the wonderful memories that I cherish from my early drive-in experiences, there is one thing that stands out in my mind. It is that brief slice of time that exists between the two movies of a double feature. I am referring to, of course, the intermission. I can remember running at a frantic pace to the concession stand shortly after the first feature's credits rolled. There I would purchase my treasures—two hot dogs, French fries, and a large soft drink. Then, racing back to the car, I would savor my snack bar goodies while watching the stream of concession trailers that were designed exclusively for drive-ins.

Today the town of Essex has changed considerably. Gone are all the old establishments—victims of the emergence of strip malls and chain stores. Thankfully, drive-in movie theaters have withstood the test of time. Although the number of drive-ins open for business is nowhere near the 4,000-plus recorded back in the late 1950s, those that are still in operation are experiencing a resurgence in popularity.

You may have to travel a bit to find a drive-in movie theater these days, but the trip is well worth the effort. The magic of those flickering images up on the screen against a starlit sky, the metallic ambiance of an in-car speaker, and the tempting aroma emanating from the snack bar are as unique and enjoyable now as they were when you were a kid.

Mark Bialek, President
The Drive-In Theatre Fan Club
Baltimore, Maryland

Filmack promotional trailer. *(Mark Bialek collection)*

Acknowledgments

Planning and writing any book is always a large undertaking. Cinema Under the Stars *was no exception. This book was made possible with the help and support of many people, to whom we are indebted.*

Mark and Kim Bialek, who listened to our idea and were always ready and willing to give us a helping hand. To Mark, especially, for writing the foreword to this book and spending many hours designing original artwork. We are grateful to both of them.

Debrean and Randy Loy, who trusted us with their precious photo collection of drive-in movie theaters.

Terry Lee Roth, for giving us some unique memorabilia as well as rare photographs.

Rob Giles, who lent us parts of his rather large collection and was always willing to come through for us in a pinch.

Ken Layton, who gave us 100 percent of his collection and then some.

Norman Currie, at Bettmann Archives, in New York, who took our deadline seriously.

Marc Wanamaker, at Bison Archives, in Los Angeles, who also took our deadline seriously.

Jim Lipuma, owner of the Galaxy and Moonlite Drive-Ins, for taking time out of his busy schedule to talk with us.

Tom Moyers, for getting us in touch with more drive-in enthusiasts.

Janet Lane, who gave us her artistic talents to recreate drive-in memories.

Mark Goodman, owner of the Route 66 Drive-In, for giving us permission to use his drive-in on the cover of our book.

Andy Thomas, a wonderful artist, who captured the Route 66 Drive-In so beautifully.

The Academy of Motion Picture Arts and Sciences, who steered us in all the right directions.

The UCLA libraries for helping us to gain a better knowledge and insight into the history of drive-in movie theaters.

The Los Angeles Public Library reference department for their patience.

To family and friends, especially our parents, whose encouragement and support is always appreciated.

Mike McKeon, who took time out from his busy schedule to take pictures for his sister, while chauffeuring her all around Los Angeles to help out with research.

Nancy Winters, whose support means so much to me.

Bob Everett, for taking pictures of Washington drive-ins.

Anne Dominion, my best friend, for her unconditional support.

Jon F. de Ojeda, for his support and who always comes through in a crisis.

Cookie and Joe, for always including me as part of their family.

Ron and Julie Pitkin, our publishers at Cumberland House, for putting our ideas into print.

And a special thanks to Bridget, Jack, Katie, Julia, Annette, Isabella and Claire . . . all the children that I love so very much. And, of course, to Madeleine.

Thanks to you all.

Cinema Under the Stars

INTRODUCTION

"While most roadside building types evolved gradually, the drive-in was deliberately invented. It took shape from a single prototype and—except for some technical improvements and minor variations in plan, construction, and decoration— has remained basically unchanged in form and function for half a century."[†]

The automobile and the motion picture industry are icons of American life. The two became the perfect match for inventor Richard M. Hollingshead Jr. when he combined them and opened the first drive-in movie theater in Camden, New Jersey, in the summer of 1933.

Hollingshead somehow knew that this type of movie theater could eventually prove successful, basing his assumption on the fact that a certain segment of the population never attended indoor movie houses. He felt confident that once his concept became a reality, people would love the idea of watching movies from inside their automobiles, and he was right.

Families were drawn to drive-in movie theaters due in part to their convenience. More than just a movie was offered to the ticket holder: There was no need to get all dressed up, you didn't have to hire a babysitter, parking was included in the price of the ticket, and dinner was just a quick walk to the concession stand. Drive-ins also became popular with teenagers because it was the ideal place to take a date or socialize with "the gang." What could be better than dinner and a movie under the stars?

Toward the latter part of the 1930s, a depressed economy and a world war were just two of the reasons for the somewhat slow development of drive-in movie theaters. All of that would change by the mid-1940s.

After the war, America flourished. With a booming economy, hoards of families flocked to the suburbs. The setting was perfect for the success of drive-ins. There was plenty of affordable, available land and the "car culture" in America was just beginning.

The 1950s was the golden age for drive-in movie theaters. More than 4,600 were opened for business during the prosperous and defining decade of the baby boom. To lure in the family trade, playgrounds were built for children while live bands entertained adults. Never mind that the movies were second-rate as was the sound quality—it was the "drive-in experience" that kept moviegoers coming back for more.

As the decade neared an end, so did the popularity of going to the drive-in. By the mid-1960s and well into the 1970s, "the drive-in experience" had

The first open-air movie theater opened in Camden, New Jersey, on June 6, 1933. *(UPI/Corbis-Bettmann)*

become somewhat tiresome. The inferior quality of the movies being shown combined with the antiquated sound system led many customers back to indoor theaters.

During the 1980s more and more drive-ins began closing down for good. Many owners jumped at the chance to sell their lots to land developers as a means of getting out of a sagging business.

From the more than 4,600 drive-ins recorded back in the 1950s, today there are fewer than 800 open for business across the country. Some drive-ins have become locations for "swap meets" during daylight hours so that their owners can recoup their losses due to poor attendance.

Yet with all its adversity and struggle, the drive-in movie theater has endured. It has withstood the test of time and has become a symbol for a public that is not quite ready to give up on its nostalgic past.

Today many drive-ins appear to be enjoying a resurgence in popularity. Owners and operators, taking pride in their establishments, are now offering Dolby sound along with first-run movie releases. What began as the idea of one man in Camden, New Jersey, has become a cultural icon for over half a century. Drive-in movie theaters have been and always will be a part of the American landscape.

"A Family at the Drive-In" *(Janet Lane)*

On his patent application dated August 6, 1932, inventor Richard M. Hollingshead Jr. described his vision of the drive-in movie theater: "My invention relates to a new and useful outdoor theater . . . whereby the transportation facilities to and from the theater are made to constitute an element of the seating facilities . . . wherein the performance, such as a motion picture show or the like, may be seen and heard from a series of automobiles so arranged in relation to the stage or screen, that the successive cars behind each other will not obstruct the view."[1]

Along with his application Hollingshead submitted charts and drawings to further explain his idea in precise detail. After a successful review Hollingshead was issued patent number 1,909,537 on May 16, 1933. The term of the patent was good for seventeen years, during which time he would be allowed to collect royalties from anyone who wanted to build and operate his or her own drive-in movie theater.

Hollingshead, along with his cousin Willie Warren Smith, formed Park-In Theaters, Inc. soon after receiving his patent, on June 1, 1933. The concept of an outdoor movie theater was fast becoming a reality for Hollingshead. Little did he know that it was his vision of the drive-in movie theater that would forever alter the American landscape and establish the drive-in as a cultural icon.

Richard M. Hollingshead Jr., inventor of the drive-in theater. *(Academy of Motion Picture Arts and Sciences)*

The son of a New Jersey manufacturer, Richard M. Hollingshead Jr. began his career working for his father's company, Whiz Auto Products, which produced and sold items used for the care and upkeep of automobiles.

Unchallenged by his general sales manager position, Hollingshead longed to start his own company. He had already decided that it would have to be the kind of business where he would be in control of operations. More importantly, he wanted his business to help promote and sell Whiz Auto Products. Leery of giving out credit, especially during a depression, Hollingshead believed that a "cash only" business would be the safest type to develop.

Looking for ways to achieve his goal, Hollingshead studied the market for inspiration and trends. His informal research led him to conclude that there were certain things that people were not willing to sacrifice even during a depression. He made a list: food, clothing, and automobiles. Upon further contemplation, and after spending an evening out at a local theater, he added "movies" to his list. The theater's manager confirmed to Hollingshead that many of his customers routinely attended the show despite their economic hardships.

Hollingshead went about developing a deluxe "Hawaiian Village" gas station. The overall design would include thatched roof buildings with gas station pumps resembling small palm trees. Adjacent to this gas station would be a restaurant and outdoor movie theater. It was Hollingshead's belief that his gas station would offer something that none other could. With the choice of a restaurant or outdoor theater, customers could either enjoy a good meal or watch a movie to pass the time while their cars were being serviced.

Realizing that business generally tended to drop off at night, Hollingshead felt confident that his business would become popular with more of an "after hours" crowd. However, as he got deeper into the development of such an establishment, he soon determined that the combination of gas station, restaurant, and outdoor theater would be too cumbersome for one location.

Hollingshead decided to focus all of his attention on developing just the outdoor theater. With movies as popular as they were, he rationalized that there had to be a logical explanation as to why certain segments of the population never attended them. He theorized, "The mother says she's not dressed; the husband doesn't want to put on his shoes; the question is what to do with the kids; then how to find a baby sitter; parking the car is difficult

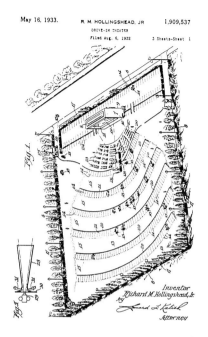

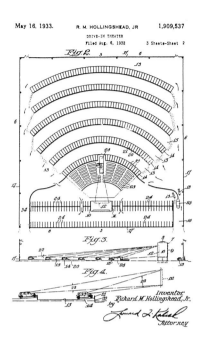

Drawings from Hollingshead's original patent application for the drive-in movie theater. *(U.S. Patent Office)*

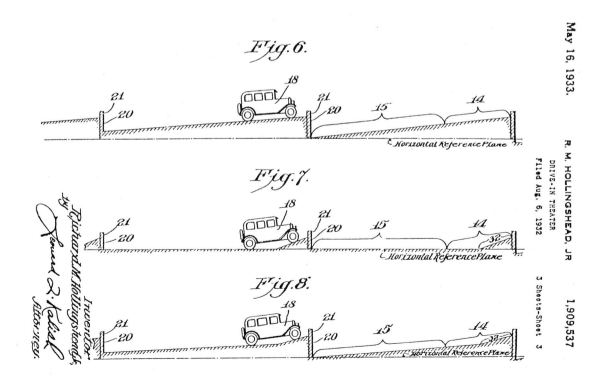

or maybe they have to pay for parking; even the seats in the theater may not be comfortable to contemplate."[2]

With those reasons in mind, Hollingshead assured himself that his idea for a drive-in movie theater had the potential to become an instant commercial success. It would also serve as a practical solution for parents who wanted to attend a movie with their children.

In the driveway of his home at 212 Thomas Avenue in Camden, New Jersey, Hollingshead began phase one of his idea by mounting a 1928 Kodak projector onto the hood of his car. From there he projected the film onto a makeshift screen, which was actually a plain white bed sheet nailed between two trees in his backyard. For sound, an ordinary radio was placed behind the sheet.

As he sat in his car watching the film, Hollingshead decided that his idea was feasible. Continuing on with his experiment, he rolled the car windows up and down to test for sound quality and turned the sprinklers on and off to recreate different weather conditions.

One problem he could already foresee was the positioning of the vehicles so that one would not obstruct another's view once they were lined up in rows. After much deliberation Hollingshead went about designing a series of ramps that would place the cars at proper angles ideal for optimum viewing. The ramps themselves would be placed on an incline and arranged in a semicircle around the screen.

With the initial design of the theater completed, Hollingshead knew that there still remained some technical details that required his immediate attention. First on his list: secure a vacant lot several acres in size that would be able to hold at least four hundred automobiles. Hollingshead located the perfect spot to erect his drive-in movie theater on Admiral Wilson Boulevard in Camden. Next, he ordered a custom built thirty-by-sixty-foot screen. Lastly, he needed to somehow develop a quality sound system. For that dilemma Hollingshead turned to his neigh-

Pico-Westwood Drive-In Movie Theater, Los Angeles, California, 1934. *(Bison Archives)*

bor in Camden, the RCA Victor Company.

RCA listened to Hollingshead's idea and came up with what they called "Controlled Directional Sound," claiming that their system would allow every patron the same volume of sound regardless of whether their car was parked in the first row or the last. The sound would be delivered from three central speakers mounted near the screen or placed in various locations around the lot.

Hollingshead also saw the need to develop a contraption that would eliminate any and all obstructions that could potentially block the screen or interfere with the picture.

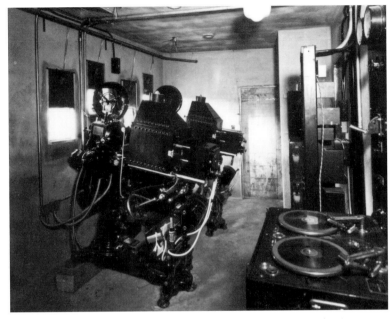

Projection booth at the Pico-Westwood theater, Los Angeles, California, 1934. *(Bison Archives)*

Specifically, he needed a way to eliminate moths and other insects that would be lured toward the white, hot lights of the projector. "In order to eliminate all insects from the path of the light from the motion picture projector . . . I provide a funnel-shaped guard directly ahead of the motion picture projector . . . and from a suitable fan or blower into a small end of the funnel . . . a clean stream of air passes through the guard funnel . . . to prevent insects from gathering . . . or approaching the lens of the projector."[3]

With many of the details nearly completed, Hollingshead was ready to begin construction of his open air theater. Looking for venture capitalists to help him out financially, Hollingshead enlisted the help of his first cousin Willie Warren Smith, who owned and operated a number of parking lots in and around the East Coast area. Together the two men formed Park-In Theaters, Inc. Shortly thereafter other investors joined Hollingshead to help him develop his drive-in movie theater.

Hollingshead premiered his new outdoor theater on June 6, 1933, just a few weeks after officially receiving his patent. The design of the Camden Drive-In would serve as a blueprint for the many thousands of outdoor theaters that followed. Outlining the drive-in's perimeter was a fence to prevent trespassers from getting a glimpse of the film for free. Planted alongside the fence were an estimated two hundred trees, some as tall as twenty feet.

Near the front entrance stood the ticket booth where cars were stopped as they entered the lot. Once occupants paid the admission fee they parked on a series of inclined ramps positioned in a semicircle in front of the screen. The projection booth was located in the middle of the first row.

On tap for the evening's main feature was *Wife Beware,* starring Adolphe Menjou. Not considered a first-run release, it nevertheless drew crowds to a packed "house." A variety of short films accompanied the film to round out the evening's entertainment. Admission was twenty-five cents per car and twenty-five cents per person. Three or more in a car were admitted for one dollar.

Coverage of the drive-in's gala grand opening swept across the country. Several news agencies reprinted a statement Hollingshead had made earlier about his new invention and the benefits it had for the public. "In the Drive-In theater one may smoke without offending others. People may

Aerial view of the Pico-Westwood Drive-In, Los Angeles, California, 1934. *(Bison Archives)*

chat or even partake of refreshments brought in their cars. . . . The Drive-In theater idea virtually transforms an ordinary motor car into a private theater box. The younger children are not permitted in movie theaters. . . . Here the whole family is welcome. . . ."[4]

Within weeks, problems began cropping up at the Camden Drive-In. Hollingshead became aware that attendance levels, which were perfectly satisfactory on weekend nights, dropped off substantially during the week. He surmised that it was because he was showing the last

The sign at the Culver City Drive-In, Southern California (1934), is an early example of the use of neon lights. *(Bison Archives)*

film at such a late hour. Patrons that had to go to work early the next morning were mostly attending on weekends. Also, neighbors living in close proximity to the drive-in complained that the noise emanating from the speakers could be heard from miles away.

In addition to all these concerns, Hollingshead was plagued with the problem of gaining access to first-run movies from major Hollywood studios for a reasonable rental fee. He did not want to continue offering second-run features to his audience. After a noble attempt to get better quality films he soon realized that his battle with the movie studios was futile. He was helpless fighting against the studio's monopoly over film distribution, which usually favored studio-owned indoor movie houses. He was left to show second- and sometimes third-run films or government-made short features.

After two years in the drive-in business, Hollingshead sold his open-air theater in Camden, wanting to spend more time licensing his patent to other would-be drive-in theater owners. However, unbeknownst to Hollingshead, other drive-in theaters had already been built in and around the northeast, in violation of his licensing agreement. Hollingshead filed a number of lawsuits against these new owners for patent infringement.

Some early drive-ins included Shankweiler's Auto Park, built in 1934, and the Weymouth Drive-In, built in 1936. Out on the west coast, the Pico-

A close-up of the "ramp" formation that allowed cars to see over one another and view the screen. Culver City Drive-In, Southern California, 1934. *(Bison Archives)*

Westwood Drive-In, near Los Angeles, opened for business in 1934, as did the Culver City Drive-In. The San Val Drive-In, located in Burbank, California, opened in 1938. None of these owners sought permission from Hollingshead for use of his patent.

The Weymouth Drive-In in Weymouth, Massachusetts, sought permission not from Hollingshead's company but from the newly formed Drive-In Theater Corporation. Hollingshead brought suit against the Drive-In Theater Corporation and fought hard to obtain the money owed to him. Eventually, Drive-In Theater Corporation entered into a licensing agreement with Park-In Theaters Inc. *Boxoffice* magazine commented, "There are already more lawsuits on drive-in theaters in this territory than there are drive-in localities."[5]

Hollingshead, continuing to file lawsuits against drive-in owners for patent infringement, began to focus his attention on drive-ins built in California. The District Court for the Southern District of California dismissed Hollingshead's claim, stating that a drive-in theater was not an invention that could be patented and thus no infringement had occurred. Upon appeal the Ninth Circuit Court ruled 2-1 that a drive-in was patentable and thus fines could be invoked against owners that didn't have the proper licensing agreement.

Elias M. Loew, owner of the Lynn Drive-In, was one of the few owners who diligently paid royalties to Hollingshead. However, he later brought suit against Park-In Theaters Inc. claiming that Hollingshead and his company did not always go after other drive-in owners who didn't have a licensing agreement. To get out of his contract with Hollingshead, Loew argued that drive-ins were not patentable and that Hollingshead could not legally collect royalties. His argument was thrown out based upon the previous ruling by the Ninth Circuit Court. Refusing to give up, Loew appealed the decision. The First Circuit Court of Appeals listened to Loew's arguments and unanimously ruled in his favor.

Their opinion read, in part, "This arcuate arrangement of parking stalls in a lot is obviously only an adaptation to automobiles of the conventional

The tall screen of the San Val Drive-In in Burbank, California (1938), dwarfs the palm trees in front of it. *(Bison Archives)*

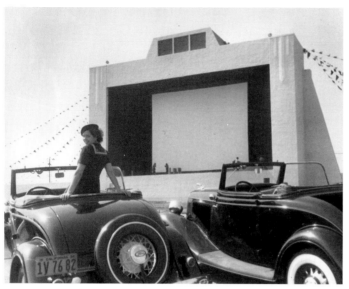

A young Southern California actress enjoys the drive-in experience. *(UPI/Corbis-Bettmann)*

The Valley Stream Drive-In on Long Island (1938) was the first open-air theater in New York state. *(UPI/Corbis-Bettmann)*

arrangement of seats in a theater employed since ancient times to enable patrons to see the performance while looking comfortably ahead in a normal sitting position without twisting the body or turning the head. . . ."[6]

Back and forth it went for Hollingshead and his company as they dealt with a hailstorm of litigation. Enraged about the reversal, Hollingshead took his case to the Supreme Court. Years after the court battles began, the high court's final ruling was against Hollingshead. It had been his last chance to seek any further legal remedies. After the court's decision Hollingshead let it be known that he had washed his hands of the motion picture industry. "There ought to be an award in the industry for ideas which built it. Like the Oscars. It might stimulate the industry. But as for me, I can assure you I'm not going to think up any more ideas for the motion picture industry. To me, the drive-in stands in the category of the greatest contribution to the industry since sound."[7]

By the late 1930s drive-in theaters, nicknamed "ozoners" by trade magazines, began cropping up around the country. However, the real success of drive-in movie theaters would not be felt for another fifteen years. Owners who saw the potential in owning one of these open-air theaters paved the way for the future.

On the West Coast, weather conditions made it possible to go to the drive-in year-round. It didn't take long for the public to take to the idea of watching a movie from the comforts of their automobile. In 1938 the experience of going to a drive-in was described in *Collier's* magazine: "Out on Pico Boulevard we located drive-in service as it neared its peak. We drove in through a tollgate, a girl seated in a booth took money for tickets, and we entered the Drive-In Theater. An usher, bearing the badge of his office—a flashlight—jumped on the running board and guided the car to a space marked out with white chalk lines. We leaned back and watched the picture shown on the open-air screen. The usher lingered on to tell us: 'We can take around five hundred cars. . . . We run two shows a night. When it rains we shut down. Our big business is during the summer. The way we keep from disturbing people is by dividing the space in sections and taking the cars to one section at a time. Yes, we charge more than most of the neighborhood houses, but people seem willing to pay.'"[8]

On June 10, 1938, the San Val opened for business in Burbank, California. Situated on ten acres of land, the drive-in could hold up to six hundred automobiles. Owners also took a stab at correcting the sound problem by hooking up speakers to individual rows of cars. It was an attempt to achieve a more even sound quality throughout the perimeter of the drive-in. The main volume switch, located in the projection booth, was controlled by an attendant who could increase or decrease the volume accordingly when a train passed by.

New York opened its first open-air theater on August 10, 1938. Despite

Refreshment service came right to patrons in their cars at the Valley Stream (1938). *(UPI/Corbis-Bettmann)*

A uniformed attendant shows patrons where to park at the Valley Stream (1938). *(UPI/Corbis-Bettmann)*

pounding sheets of rain and gusty winds, a crowd of six hundred attended the Valley Stream Drive-In's opening night.

Following the success of these drive-ins and a handful of others, more theaters were soon constructed around the country. Although progress would slow considerably due in part to the Great Depression and the war in Europe, by the end of the decade more than fifty open-air theaters would be open for business. Movie-trade insiders, though skeptical about any long-term success for drive-in movie theaters, saw the upstarts as major problems for well-established indoor houses. Indeed, "They [drive-ins] are getting more in the way of regularly operated theaters and causing theater men to raise complaints about which seemingly nothing is done."[9]

8-Mile Drive-In, Detroit, Michigan, 1938. *(Bison Archives)*

Instead of joining forces with drive-in owners, indoor theater owners began to battle it out with them over audience share and admission fees, due to the fact that children were admitted for free at many drive-ins. Indoor houses were used to generating healthy profits by virtue of a studio-run monopoly over film distribution. They were not about to change a system that was working so well for them. By refusing to give drive-ins first-run releases, the studios believed that they had sealed their fate and assumed that the drive-in movie theater would be a short-lived phenomenon. Nothing could have prepared either side for the explosion that would occur in the next decade.

Customers drive in to the drive-in, 1938. *(UPI/Corbis-Bettmann)*

The drive-in movie theater had made its mark in the 1930s. Despite the Hollywood studios' attempts to disassociate themselves from it, the drive-in's popularity soared in the 1940s as the public's acceptance of this new-found recreation grew to new heights.

Front entrance to Shankweiler's. *(Debrean and Randy Loy collection)*

Shankweiler's Drive-In, located in Orefield, Pennsylvania, is the oldest drive-in theater still in existence. It has been in continuous operation since opening on April 15, 1934.

It was 1933 when Wilson Shankweiler, vacationing in Atlantic City, New Jersey, came upon Richard Hollingshead's Camden Drive-In theater. A devout movie buff, Shankweiler studied the layout and operation of Hollingshead's theater. Upon returning home he went about setting up his own outdoor theater by converting a landing strip behind his Shankweiler Hotel into a makeshift drive-in. According to *Boxoffice* magazine, "Back in the old barnstorming days, the pilots would fly in there for Shankweiler Hotel's famous chicken and waffles dinner. A circle of white gravel on the edge of the theater's parking spaces was used by the pilots to help determine sufficient landing and take-off room."[1]

The original screen consisted of a sheet hung between two poles. The film was viewed from a 16-mm projector that sat on a table, while the audio sound was provided through a large horn, set up as a speaker.

As more people began to patronize Shankweiler's new theater, the town counsel levied an amusement tax against all theaters. Shortly thereafter, Shankweiler proudly posted a sign at the entrance that read, "Free Movies. Parking 50 cents," cleverly avoiding having to pay the amusement tax.

Established as "Shankweiler's Auto Park," the theater has survived through the years in an industry plagued by social and economic changes. After sustaining a damaged screen and projection booth when a hurricane hit the area in 1955, Shankweiler's was rebuilt and remodeled.

Owner Bob Malkames sees drive-ins as more of a hobby than a business venture. "My drive-in is going to be there as long as I'm around. We're in good shape."[2]

An attendant works the concession stand at Shankweiler's.
(Debrean and Randy Loy collection)

Two youngsters at Shankweiler's enjoy a movie as generations have before them.
(Debrean and Randy Loy collection)

"Woman Handing Out Tickets" *(Janet Lane)*

In the early 1940s, the United States was still in the throes of the Great Depression and the unemployment rate soared. Despite this, drive-in movie theaters were making their presence known. Although the quality of the sound, picture, and the film itself at most drive-ins paled in comparison to indoor theaters, Americans fell in love with the idea of seeing a motion picture show while sitting in their car.

Owners of drive-ins began reporting an increase in weekly profits. As business continued to grow, anyone who owned a drive-in could easily make a comfortable living from their initial investment. The cost of opening a new drive-in ranged from $25,000 to $75,000, depending upon the location. Richard Hollingshead had built his Camden Drive-In for $60,000.

Thomas Pryor of the *New York Times* observed, "Ranging in size from a capacity of 250 cars to more than 1,000, the average drive-in, on the basis of two persons to a car, can accommodate an audience approximately as large as the normal size theater. The one disadvantage is that the drive-in is largely a seasonal affair. However, the fellow with a good location is not too much concerned about that for he can make enough hay in the summer months to pass the winter comfortably in Florida."[1]

In May of 1941 Chicago opened its first drive-in theater. Built at a cost of $75,000, it was one of the biggest open-air theaters with a lot size of twenty acres, and it could hold more than 1,100 cars. Admission was forty cents for adults and twenty cents for children. Cars were escorted into the lot by usherettes riding bicycles. Attendants were available to service patrons' vehicles by checking the oil, gas, water, and air.

Drive-in theaters around the country were doing so well that owners often didn't see the need to improve the quality of their facilities. Wooden-framed screens in need of paint or repair due to harsh weather conditions were left untouched. The sound quality was still considered second-rate, as were the movies being featured. Unpaved lots spewed forth clouds of dust and dirt. Poorly built outhouses often served as the only available restroom facility.

Despite all these factors, the moviegoing public kept pouring in through the ticket booths. Owners counting their nightly receipts clearly didn't see the need to upgrade since business was already good. They noted that their customers preferred going to the drive-in because it was convenient and not because of the quality of the facility.

The small percentage of owners who did upgrade and improve the atmosphere at their theaters focused on a more practical aspect—the concession stand. By the mid-1940s, the concession stand became a mainstay for the success of any drive-in facility. In addition to ticket sales, food sales was considered another sure way to increase profits. While the majority of drive-ins offered snacks purchased at a central location, larger drive-ins experimented with ushers delivering orders of soft drinks and the like directly to the customer's vehicle.

Some owners made noticeable improvements such as paving their lots to cut back on

Advertisement for the Silver Lake Drive-In emphasizing all the pluses of the drive-in experience. *(Mark Bialek collection)*

the amount of dust and dirt spewing into the air. Others opted to spray insecticides to help reduce the mosquito population, which plagued customers nightly.

Despite the drive-in's sudden growth in popularity, there were problems. Drive-in theaters were often criticized by Hollywood trade magazines as just another passing fancy. Indoor theater owners still complained that drive-ins were taking business away from their own theater chains, especially since drive-ins were admitting children for free. As Thomas Pryor in the *New York Times* noted, "To the regular theater man who doesn't operate one, the drive-in is regarded as a nuisance and unfair competition."[2]

Sound quality was another major problem. Because sound was provided by just a few speakers that had to reach every car in the lot, residents living around a drive-in complained about the noise level. Entire neighborhoods took drive-in owners to court, where it was declared a misdemeanor if sound could be heard at a distance of fifty feet from the property line. An attempt at solving the problem of sound quality was made in 1941 when RCA developed the in-car speaker, which allowed individual sound control. But it wouldn't be until 1946, after the war, that the system would be implemented by every drive-in across the country.

Drive-in theaters also became the cause for many traffic tie-ups due to long lines of cars waiting to enter the lot, which often blocked nearby streets for miles, attracting the attention of local authorities.

The most common complaint, according to the *Motion Picture Herald,* was "that drive-ins are built too close to the highways, thereby causing traffic congestion at the points where the cars enter or leave the grounds. In some states operators have consulted with officials, but this cooperation has not been uniform everywhere."[3] To help solve this problem, entrance roads were implemented to act as holding areas for cars waiting to enter the theater's lot.

Industry observers still doubted any long term

Early drive-in movie theater; note the fence to keep out curious non-paying onlookers. *(Bison Archives)*

potential for the drive-in. *Boxoffice* magazine dismissed drive-in movie theaters altogether when they compiled their list of new theaters opening nationwide: "Drive-in theaters cropped up in a number of sections during the past year and in the main, have been eliminated from this survey, since there is no permanency to such open air projects in contrast with regular theaters."[4]

Plans for large scale drive-ins soon halted due to the war. Owners readily complied with government restrictions for gas rationing and the use of any rubber products, since both were scarce during war years. The public was asked to curtail all pleasure driving, which included driving out to the nearest drive-in. In fact, attendance was down for both indoor and outdoor theaters, but none closed down.

One major problem that drive-in owners continued to face was the quality of films made available to them. Just as Richard Hollingshead had tried and

The massive 125-foot screen at this New York drive-in towers over the woman in front of it. *(Bison Archives)*

On nights when they didn't go to the drive-in, kids could play this game; 1948. *(Robert Giles collection)*

failed to gain access to first-run films for his Camden theater, drive-in owners began to battle it out with Hollywood themselves for the same reason.

Determined to fight for the right to show first-run films at their theaters, owners would soon face Hollywood's powers that be. Drive-in theater owners took on the "Big Five" studios: Paramount, Twentieth Century Fox, Warner Brothers, MGM, and RKO. These five studios produced 95 percent of the "A" quality films released.

Other smaller, independent studios, such as Columbia, United Artists, and Universal, were generally releasing "B" quality productions—spaghetti westerns, detective stories, and romance films.

Drive-ins were, for the most part, limited to showing films from these independent studios, and the film rental costs were still extremely high.

Drive-in owners cited unfair competition with indoor theater chains, which were owned and run by the studios. Their claim was that indoor theaters had an unfair advantage in gaining access to first-run film releases.

Lawsuits filed against the studios went all the way to the Supreme Court. The high court broke up the monopoly, stating that all five major studios had to sell off their theater holdings. By law, films were to be distributed fairly to everyone. This decision, the high court determined, would help to make the motion picture industry more competitive.

Fred Hift of the *Motion Picture Herald* noted, "Most of the major companies now license their films to a drive-in only after the operator has agreed to pay at least a certain portion of the product on percentage terms in order to gauge the business he is doing."[5] Major film companies told drive-in owners that they were being treated like any other theater that they did business with. "If they ask for a certain run, and if they can prove they can pay for it, we consider the request."[6]

In 1946 there were 102 drive-in movie theaters operating across the country. By 1949 that number would jump to 1,000. "The rapid growth of the drive in has left veteran showmen wide-eyed with amazement," commented the *New York Times*.[7] It seemed as if drive-ins could hardly be built fast enough. More families were moving out of the crowded cities and into the suburbs where there was plenty of wide open land. The traditional Sunday drive was now being replaced with a trip to the drive-in.

Some developers requesting permits to build their own drive-in were being turned down by zoning commissions "for reasons ranging from fear of traffic congestion to complaints over noise."[8] Drive-ins located near and around larger cities had the most difficulty with zoning boards, whereas in states where there was plenty of wide open space available, drive-ins continued to sprout up unabated.

For those who did get the go-ahead to build an outdoor theater the timing was perfect. Land was readily available and still cheap to buy, and America's love affair with the car showed no signs of winding down. The *Motion Picture Herald* said at the time, "The Drive-In Theater, the screen's institution of the far-flung crossroads of the nation, impeded by war economy, is hastening to catch up with the motor age of which it is essentially a product."[9]

Drive-in movie theaters were fast becoming the ideal place for families with children. What owners sold to the public was not the picture but an

entire package of amenities. Despite the fact that the films were mainly second-run releases, moviegoers still loved the convenience more than anything
else. It was the novelty of knowing that one could pack the family into the
car and enjoy a night out, never having to get out of the car until arriving
back at home.

Along with this new surge in open-air theaters came an onslaught of
commercial products made specifically for drive-ins. Almost overnight there
were in-car heaters, new speaker systems, and newer popcorn machine models for concession stands. Other products included a glycerin solution for
windshields to ward off rain and the "Car-Net," which consisted of "sec-
tioned screens" for the windows to keep out insects and other unwanted
pests.

previous page: A wooden nickel from the Moon Glo Theatre gave the bearer a bargain on the next visit.
(Robert Giles collection); above: A typical carload at an early drive-in—teens on a date. *(Bison Archives)*

this page: Postcard and business card from Route 66 Drive-In, Carthage, Missouri; *next page:* Brochure handed out to patrons at Route 66 Drive-In. *(Mark Goodman collection)*

Owners, noticing the increase in the drive-in's popularity, began competing with one another to gain their share of audience attendance. Suddenly, drive-in services were booming. There were bottle-warming tables, flat tire repair and a pre-movie car wash. Some theaters went so far as to do your laundry during the movie. Still others offered to do your weekly shopping and deliver your groceries to your car if you brought them your grocery list.

Some theaters still had mechanics that would check the oil and tire pressure and others had ushers that rode along the sideboard of the car and guided it into the parking space. Owners tried to out-do their competitors by offering more individual services—anything to keep their customers coming back.

Fred Hift of the *Motion Picture Herald* noted, "The size of the drive-in staff varies, depending somewhat on the car capacity of the establishment. Attendants are on hand to sell soft-drinks and candy, along with hot dogs and other food items. Others may hawk ice-cream and drinks among the parked cars. Still others are detailed to the playground to supervise the activities of the children. Some drive-ins are required by the zoning boards to

V. F. Naramore & W. D. Bradfield

Welcome You To

Carthage's

Newest Form of Motion Picture Ententainment

"66"

Drive-In Theatre

One Mile West of Carthage on Highway 66 and 71

**Family Entertainment
Under the Stars**

How To Best Handle Your In-Car Speaker

After parking, your in-car speaker is within arm's reach. Place speaker on car window or door frame just below window. You will find a volume control on the speaker and you may adjust sound to suit your own precise need. In leaving, please do not start motor until you have replaced speaker.

These in-car speakers are the finest available but like any mechanical equipment require careful handling to remain in perfect condition. We solicit your cooperation.

If you should accidently drive off with a speaker, please return to us as these speakers are manufactured so that they cannot be used for any other purpose than drive-in theatres.

Thanks For Coming — Hurry Back

Program Policy . . .

Opening Time of Box Office
Each evening at 6:30 P.M.

Two Shows Nightly
First show starts at dark.
Two complete shows nightly.

Rain or Clear
The 66 Drive-In Theatre will present shows each and every night, regardless of weather . . . Rain will not affect your vision . . . Individual speaker in your car enables you to hear with windows closed.

Children FREE at all Times
There is no admission charge for children under 12. Adult admission is 50c per person including State and Federal Taxes.

Program Changes
See the Daily Papers for our attractions.
Feature attractions are carefully selected to entertain the whole family. New shows every Sunday, Wednesday and Friday. A COLOR CARTOON ON EVERY PROGRAM. . . And Short Comedies, Sportlights, and other novelties make up a two-hour program.

Privacy and Comfort
These are yours when you attend the 66 Drive-In. Ideal for shut-ins, children and elderly people. . . Dress as you please. . . Smoke, talk . . . Take refreshments, all without disturbing others.

REPLACE SPEAKER BEFORE STARTING CAR!

For Your Information . . .

Refreshment Stand
Our DeLuxe Refreshment Stand is located in the center of the fourth ramp. A center roadway, marked with the Ramp in which you are PARKED, makes it easy to find your way to and from the stand.
Here you may enjoy Delicious Hot Dogs, Ice Cold Drinks, Popcorn, Ice Cream, Novelties and many other treats.

No Charges for your Car
And no parking worries when you attend the 66 Drive-In Theatre.
Don't dressup, come as you are, eat, smoke, drink, chew, if you like.

Free Playground for Children
The Children's Playground will be directly in front of screen. This will be built this fall and will be in operation for next season.

Location of Rest Rooms
These are located on the sides of the Refreshment Building in the center of the area.

Come or go at Anytime
You can enter or leave the 66 Drive-In without obstructing the view of others. When leaving, FIRST, REPLACE SPEAKER, drive forward, turn RIGHT to exit roadway. Follow directions of signs and attendants.

Drive Carefully
Remember, there are always many children in the Theatre Area. It takes only 10 seconds more to reach the exit at 5 to 10 miles per hour than at 10 to 15 miles per hour. Don't risk a life or serious injury for 10 seconds.

REPLACE SPEAKER BEFORE STARTING CAR!

This drive-in theater in Salsbury, Massachusetts, has a slightly more elaborate screen. *(Bison Archives)*

hire their own deputy sheriff to keep the traffic flowing smoothly in and out of the theater without causing a congestion on the highway."[10]

Along with the screen, speaker poles, and snack bar there were soon picnic tables, barbecue pits, shuffleboard, and playgrounds added to the landscape of the drive-in movie theater. Uniformed attendants looked after children as they played on the playground equipment. Some drive-ins went so far as to bring in live circus acts and dog and pony shows. A few drive-ins offered a kennel service for patrons' pets. "For older folks who may not want to watch the show, some drive-ins have patios where they can sit and sip a cool drink before, during or after the show," reported the *Motion Picture Herald.*[11]

The cost of building an outdoor theater had reached $75,000 to $100,000 by 1948. And that was before adding all of the child-friendly amenities—a must to bring in family business—which boosted the cost by about $20,000.

Industry observers, noting the type of customer that attended drive-ins, determined that the average audience was made up of families with children who would probably never attend movies at an indoor theater. Fortunately for the drive-in owner, there was no shortage of families with small children during the postwar years of the late 1940s. The new challenge was how to bring in these families long before the first feature was shown on the screen.

Owners sought to motivate customers by offering them even more amenities. They began creating a carnival-like atmosphere to help stir up their customers' appetites so that more time and—more importantly—money would be spent at the concession stand.

Time magazine observed, "They woo the family trade with an imposing sideshow of picnic areas, merry-go-rounds, dance floors, shuffleboard courts, and bottle-warming, car-washing and laundry service. Among the latest gimmicks, planned or already drawing customers to the airers: nightclubs, golf driving ranges, Shetland ponies, barbecue pits and motorized bingo (the jackpot goes to the right speedometer mileage)."[12]

Advertising for drive-in theaters came from radio spots, blimps, billboards, postcards, and matchbook covers. Owners often partnered with local clubs and organizations to increase publicity. But the most important advertising came from the drive-ins themselves. The big towering screen that faced the highway could be seen for miles as motorists sped along the interstate. Because it was on display twenty-four hours a day, owners made sure they kept up the screen's appearance. Some owners took it upon themselves to create a new and sometimes stunning roadside attraction that didn't neces-

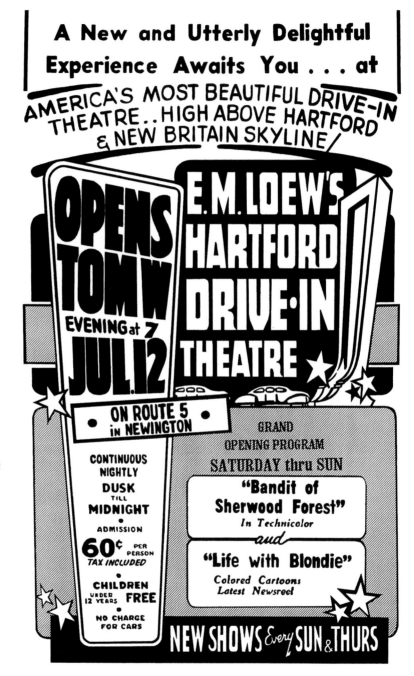

Advertisement for Loew's Hartford Drive-In. *(Mark Bialek collection)*

Advertisements aimed at drive-in owners in *Boxoffice* magazine, 1947.
(Author's collection)

sarily have to do with their drive-in. Others saw it as a free opportunity to show off their theater, so they painted the name of their establishment or commissioned artists to design a logo or theme for their theater on the back of the screen. In his book, *Main Street to Miracle Mile,* Chester Liebs writes, "Screen tower back panels were often enlivened with flamboyant displays featuring mimetic or regional images. The Rodeo Theater (1949) in Tucson, for example, boasted a cowgirl

Without cars, the Harbor Drive-In in National City, California (1949), looks like a pretty bleak place. *(Bison Archives)*

twirling a neon lasso; the Tropicaire in Miami (1949) had a giant planter filled with flood-lit live palm trees built on the tower; while San Diego's Campus Drive-In (1948) featured a gigantic cheerleader, still extant, brilliantly outlined in a neon kaleidoscope of colors."[13]

Owners kept in mind that it was the environment at the drive-in, not the movie, that was the real draw. Some interesting drive-ins designed around that concept were seen as oddities. For example, in early June 1948, Ed Brown, a former Navy flier, opened the world's first "fly-in, drive-in." The theater, located in Asbury Park, New Jersey, could accommodate up to 500 cars and 25 airplanes. The *Motion Picture Herald* described this unique theater: "The aircraft landing on the airstrip adjoining the drive-in are taxied up to a ramp facing the screen and are equipped with speakers to enable the pilot and the passenger to hear and see the show from the cabin of the plane. A jeep service is provided to haul the plane back to the takeoff strip."[14]

Lighting became another important aspect of the drive-in. Bulbs that emanated blue and red light were placed on top of poles in and around the drive-in's perimeter. They replicated moonlight, casting an eerie halo of color. The lights did not disturb the projection of the film, and they added a certain ambiance to the darkness of the theater. The main advantage of the lights, though, was their practicality—patrons could now find their way around the lot, especially to the concession stand and back to their car, without the aid of a flashlight. The lights also allowed cars to leave the lot without the use of headlights. Neon was already becoming a trademark for the drive-in's exterior decor, so it was a natural transition to have these lights added to the interior.

By the end of the 1940s anyone interested in owning a drive-in only had to pay for the privilege. Many companies offered package deals: "companies like RCA, and many others, did everything involved from site selection to construction to opening night. All the new owner had to do was hand over the money, then show up on opening night to take over the running of the place."[15]

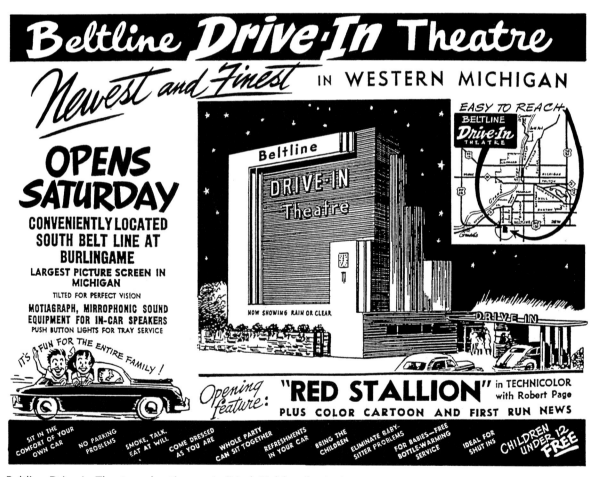

Beltline Drive-In Theatre advertisement. *(Mark Bialek collection)*

In early 1949, the Drive-In Movie Association and drive-in theater own-ers lobbied Congress—unsuccessfully—against instituting daylight savings time. Theater owners did not relish the prospect of longer days in the sum-mer, forcing the first show of the evening back to as late as 9:00 P.M. Owners felt that showing films that late would hurt attendance.

While many in Hollywood still did not approve of the drive-in movie the-ater concept, there was a small majority who were finally beginning to recog-nize their benefits in the industry. William Rogers, vice president in charge of sales at MGM, said, "If they [drive-ins] are catering to people who seldom went to theaters, and if they are giving service to young parents with small children, or folks who heretofore have had difficulties because of infirmities to attend theaters regularly, certainly we should give them every encourage-ment as another department of the motion-picture industry."[16]

The growth of drive-ins across the country showed few signs of slowing down. Some owners feared that the industry might somehow be harmed by the propagation of outlets, but it was in fact only the beginning. Still to come was the decade of the 1950s, the "golden age" of the drive-in. The *New York Times* noted, "No one in the movie business appears to know what the country's capacity for drive-in theaters might be, but there are indications galore that this building program is just about approaching high gear."[17]

"Snack Bar Guy" *(Janet Lane)*

At the Snack Bar

The business of selling food from a concession stand was not fully realized during the early development of drive-in movie theaters. Owners, tending to focus more on profits made through ticket sales rather than food items, could not justify the cost of running a full service snack bar. Also, many owners made the assumption that their patrons had already eaten their evening meal before coming out to the drive-in or that they were bringing in their own supplies of food and drink to enjoy during the film.

Although Richard Hollingshead Jr. did sell beer and sandwiches from a makeshift counter at the Camden Drive-In, it was more of an afterthought. Hollingshead waited a week after his grand opening before installing this early "concession stand." Besides, like later owners, he assumed that if any money was to be made, it would be through ticket sales rather than food.

Drive-ins that did sell drinks, along with a limited variety of snack items, did so mainly as a courtesy to their customers. Little or no thought was given to the design of the concession stand. Many were nothing more than small, rustic shacks where items were sold through an open window. Far from the focal point it would later become, the early concession stand was often placed in the back of the lot's perimeter or near the front entrance, next to the ticket

Filmack trailers were fun and enticing.
(Mark Bialek collection)

booth. Some larger drive-ins had two stands located at opposite ends of the lot for the convenience of patrons.

The San Val Drive-In, in Southern California, was one of the first early drive-ins to go beyond serving customers from a makeshift counter or window and set up a permanent building for their concession sales. Kerry Seagrave, in his book, *Drive-In Theaters: A History From Their Inception in 1933,* writes, "The concession building was rudimentary and illustrated the small role concessions played in most early drive-ins. Housing a hot-water heater, gas range and a few appliances, this building was only 10 by 18, with a six stool counter."[1]

In the early 1940s, drive-in owners began expanding their concession business. Progress was slow but owners eventually realized that sales made from their concession stand could increase their profit margins by as much as forty percent. By the mid-1940s it was apparent that a well-run concession stand was a mandatory element in the success of any drive-in movie theater. "Take away its confectionery sales profits and the average drive-in theater would probably fold in a fortnight," predicted *Boxoffice* magazine in 1945.[2]

Noting that indoor theaters made most of their money at their snack bars, drive-in owners soon began to heavily promote their concession stands to hungry movie-goers. The practice of letting children in for free was now about to pay off in a big way for owners. Rising concession sales were largely attributed to children, mainly because they were often accompanied by a parent who was also likely to make a purchase.

The rush was on for owners to design a concession stand that was appealing to their customers. It would have to be a place that was clean, comfortable, and appetizing. It also had to draw in hungry customers between features.

Most drive-ins developed the "single station" concession stand. Customers lined up and gave their order to the concessions attendant, who then filled the order and handed the items to the customer. While this system worked rather well for smaller drive-ins, some larger facilities tried to come up with a system that would allow everyone service during the

above and below: Stills from Filmack trailers. *(Mark Bialek collection)*

fifteen-minute intermission, during which time the vast majority of concession sales took place.

The Park Drive-In in Greensborough, North Carolina, devised the "talk back" system. When a customer bought his ticket he was handed a menu listing the usual drive-in fare: hamburgers, hot dogs, sandwiches, ice cold sodas, ice cream, and popcorn. At any time during the film the moviegoer could press a button located on the speaker pole and place his order through a microphone. The order was then promptly filled and delivered fresh and hot to the car. Although innovative, this system was not successful since it required extra wiring to be installed. It was an expensive proposition that failed.

For other large drive-in owners, it soon became obvious that there often wasn't enough time to serve every customer if everyone

rushed to eat during intermission, so they tried to come up with alternatives. Some owners built children's playgrounds on the premises. They hoped that this would entice families to get to the drive-in at a much earlier hour, where they would eat their evening meal before watching the movie. The *New York Times* reported, "By bringing the family groups out an hour or so before show time the candy, ice cream, popcorn, soda, coffee, hot-dog and hamburger stands among other concessions do a thriving business. According to reports, it is not unusual for receipts from these enterprises to range in amount from 40 to 60 percent of the gross box office revenue."[3]

Another way owners attempted to get families to the drive-in earlier was by building a dance floor in the space in front of the screen. Owners hired live musicians in hopes that moviegoers would arrive early and work up hearty appetites out on the dance floor.

More ideas were implemented to eliminate the fifteen-minute dash for food and to keep moviegoers snacking throughout the evening. Some larger drive-ins tried making their concession stands more personable by hiring carhops. Still others had attendants walk around the lot pushing heavy carts loaded down with food and drinks.

Although these conveniences were appreciated by customers, the majority of owners still opted to sell food directly from a central location because, after all, the extra services cost extra money, and most theater owners made a tidy profit from concessions just by making the most of the fifteen-minute rush.

The concession business could be run one of two ways: It could be fully operated by the owner of the drive-in, or it could be leased to a concessionaire, or an outside company that took full control of the snack bar, from ordering supplies to serving food. According to the *Motion Picture Herald,* "There are two lines of thinking on the drive-in sale of popcorn, candy, drinks and the like. In some theaters, attendants wander between the rows of parked cars, offering their wares in a loud voice. This is said to insure a higher sales volume, but at the same time it drives away the better-type patrons. Other drive-ins, and these seem to be in the majority, prefer customers to purchase confections and soft drinks at stands set up at the side of the field."[4]

An owner could expect anywhere from 25 to 30 percent of the gross receipts if he decided to lease out his snack bar. If he took it upon himself to run the entire operation, then the percentage from gross receipts could jump as high as 40 percent. For every dollar spent through the selling of tickets, forty-five cents was made from selling food, and "[a]ny loss at the gate was more than made up for at the concession stand."[5]

Another way drive-in owners promoted their concessions was by advertising their goodies in a series of film trailers shown during the intermission. Many of these trailers were produced and distributed exclusively for drive-in movie theaters by companies whose products were sold at the snack bar.

Armour Foods of Chicago was one such company. It produced a series of one-minute trailers for its products, reminding the audience to "Stretch your legs and perk up with a cooling drink, a box of popcorn, and a delicious Armour Star Frank on a bun."[6]

Filmack Studios was a company that developed and distributed thousands of intermission trailers made exclusively for the drive-in movie theater. Located in Chicago, Filmack created such classic images as dancing hot dogs and a chorus line of popcorn boxes, ice cream sandwich bars, ice cold sodas, and candy bars. Filmack's trailers also relayed pertinent information, such as when the next feature would begin, and reminders to remove the car speaker before backing out of the parking space. Owners noticed an increase in hot dog sales immediately following the showing of one of these trailers, as compared to when no trailer was used at all.

Over 80 percent of drive-ins used these trailers in one form or another. Those that didn't show the trailers had an attendant walk among the cars and tempt patrons by calling out reminders that intermission was a great time to buy snack bar items.

To increase the window of time in which patrons could purchase food and drinks, some drive-in owners ran a newsreel or cartoon just before or after the intermission. They felt this would help give people time to get back to their cars before the second feature began.

At drive-ins where carhops were not employed, owners discovered that often when a customer came in contact with the full display of snack bar goodies at the con-

Filmack produced many of the ever popular dancing snack bar goodies trailers. *(Mark Bialek collection)*

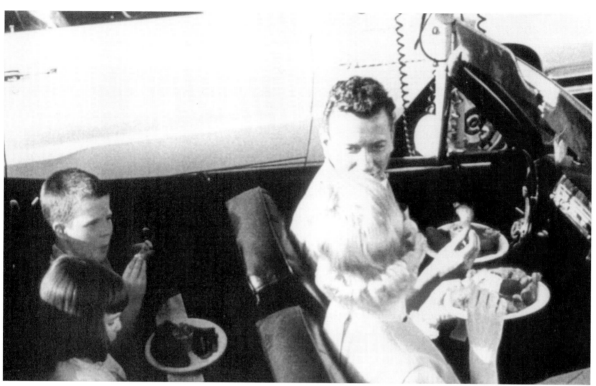

Filmack trailer showing the target drive-in audience, a family. *(Mark Bialek collection)*

cession stand, he or she was apt to buy more. Larger drive-ins offered a tram service so that customers didn't have to walk to and from their automobiles.

Food sold at drive-ins soon became familiar to moviegoers. Items such as popcorn, hot dogs, candy, and ice cream were standard for all drive-in movie theaters. Larger drive-ins, open for business year round, offered a full dinner menu for their patrons, and could justify the cost of installing a full kitchen.

Along with the food, some drive-ins offered assorted sundries such as Kleenex, comic books, and toys. Some, as described in the *Motion Picture Herald,* went so far as to have a nurse on duty, who usually had a small station set up inside the concession building. "You've got your baby along? There are drive-ins that have a nurse on duty to watch the youngster and even to prepare his formula with just the right temperature."[7]

As the popularity of the concession stand grew, owners developed different ways to make the building more appealing. Some planted a grassy knoll in front lined with flowers. Others set up an adjacent outdoor eating area. "Picnic tables were often found around the concession stand. It was felt that these tables, with people sitting at them, prompted other patrons to get out of their cars and head for the snack bar."[8]

By the 1950s, a few drive-ins were offering such exotic fare as Chinese egg rolls and pizza. In fact, the drive-in was the only place in town to buy a pizza because at that time there were no pizza parlors. Often people would pay the admission price for the drive-in just to purchase a pizza, opting not to stay for the movie.

Vending machines, placed inside snack bars, also served the owner well. Like the concession stand itself, the machines targeted young patrons because owners knew that children were apt to carry coins and not paper money. These self-serve machines were a perfect diversion for any child who was making a trip to the restroom without the aid of a parent.

By the mid-1950s the "look" of the concession stand had changed dramatically for some drive-in theaters. Owners who chose to rebuild or remodel opted for the "cafeteria," or self-serve, style snack bar developed and designed by Al Gordon, the president of a hotel and restaurant equipment company. This kind of snack bar cut down on the number of employees

Filmack snack bar trailers. *(Mark Bialek collection)*

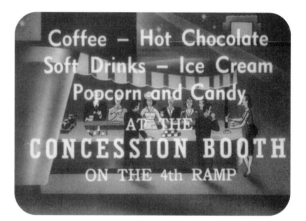

Obviously, owners were pushing the concession stand pretty hard with these Filmack trailers.
(Mark Bialek collection)

needed to serve customers, and also shortened the amount of time customers spent in line during the intermission.

"In our experience, we have discovered that the cafeteria style counter is vastly superior to the older type of front counter service. In theaters holding from 600 to 1000 cars, the four-lane cafeteria should be installed. The four lanes should be identical, each serving the same wares, preferably with turnstiles at the beginning of each lane for protection against pilfering," Gordon observed.[9]

Gordon claimed that it was his company that designed the turnstile used by many restaurants. The turnstile was especially beneficial for drive-ins because patrons could not enter the line without being noticed by a cashier. Gordon saw the drive-in as a magnet for families: "The lights and signs on the marquees sometimes prove a magnet to draw them inside and the concessions can be an irresistible lure. It has been proved that the title of the motion picture attraction on the marquee is sometimes of lesser importance than the offerings sold in the concession building."[10]

With new and improved snack bars in place, owners were beginning to reap the rewards of selling food. Concession areas were being promoted just as much as, if not more than, the films themselves.

Concession stand with traditional neon lights at the Holiday Drive-In, Hamilton, Ohio. *(Terry Lee Roth collection)*

"It's a meal in itself!" *(Filmack trailer from the Mark Bialek collection)*

Advertisement for Filmack, makers of many of the animated trailers that contributed to the drive-in experience. *(Author's collection)*

Mark Bialek collection

Drive-in owners hoped that these trailers would induce patrons to make the walk to the concession stand and buy treats. *(Mark Bialek collection)*

A reminder of the drive-in's heyday in the 1950s, this colorful sign marks the entrance to the Greater Pittsburgh Five Drive In Theatres. *(Terry Lee Roth collection)*

The Route 110 Drive-In Theatre on Long Island had a "fabulous" playground with a railroad. *(Author's collection)*

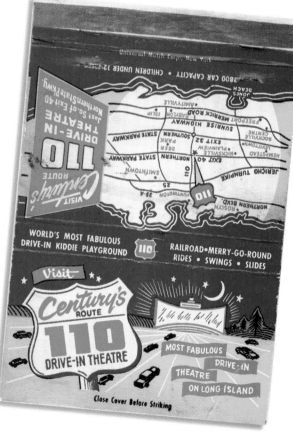

Mark Bialek collection

above: The Moon Glo Drive-In gave patrons these wooden nickels, good for a discount on tickets or concessions. *(Robert Giles collection)*
left: After drive-in owners hit upon the idea of broadcasting the sound of the movies over AM radio, these speakers became harder to find, but in the golden age of the drive-in, they were at every theater. *(Michael McKeon collection)*

The inside of this 1948 matchbook from the Weymouth Drive-In in Weymouth, Massachusetts, cautions: "Due to the Sensational Nature of the Picture it is Recommended for ADULTS ONLY." *(Author's collection)*

The combination of the drive-in experience and the famed highway makes the Route 66 Drive-In Theatre a real slice of Americana. *(Mark Goodman collection)*

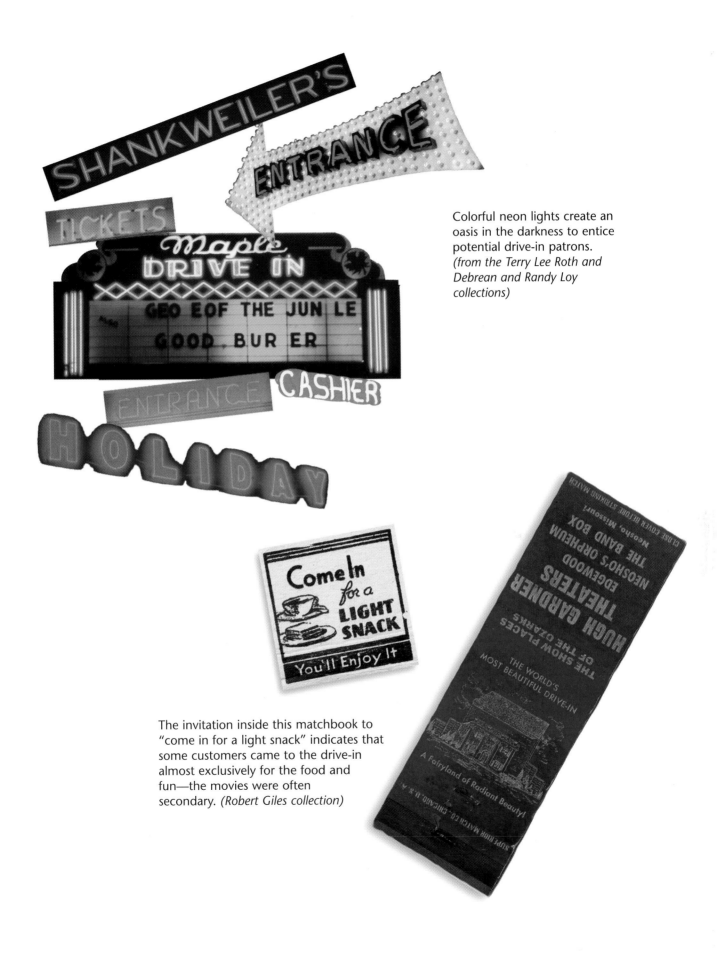

Colorful neon lights create an oasis in the darkness to entice potential drive-in patrons. *(from the Terry Lee Roth and Debrean and Randy Loy collections)*

SHANKWEILER'S

ENTRANCE

TICKETS

Maple **DRIVE IN**

GEO E OF THE JUN LE

GOOD BUR ER

ENTRANCE **CASHIER**

HOLIDAY

Come In *for a* **LIGHT SNACK** You'll Enjoy It

The invitation inside this matchbook to "come in for a light snack" indicates that some customers came to the drive-in almost exclusively for the food and fun—the movies were often secondary. *(Robert Giles collection)*

THE BAND BOX

NEOSHO'S ORPHEUM

EDGEWOOD

HUGH GARDNER THEATERS

THE SHOW PLACES OF THE OZARKS

Neosho, Missouri!

THE WORLD'S MOST BEAUTIFUL DRIVE-IN

A Fairyland of Radiant Beauty!

Mark Bialek collection

Mark Bialek collection

Mark Bialek collection

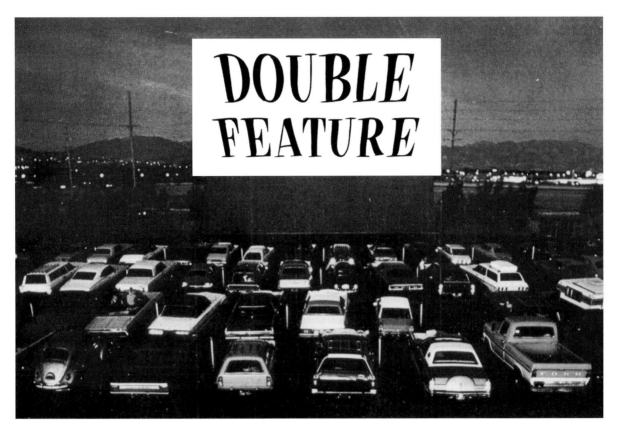

DOUBLE FEATURE

" From its novelty state of just a few years ago the drive-in theater has mushroomed into a multi-million dollar outlet for the exhibition of motion pictures. From Maine to California increasing numbers of Americans are taking in the movies with nary a thought about bus schedules or 'where are we going to park the car'? They just drive into a fan-shaped arena dominated by a towering motion picture screen and see the show while seated in the family automobile."[1]

Indeed, by the early 1950s it was apparent that Americans had come to fully accept the drive-in movie theater as the place to go for wholesome, family entertainment. This ringing endorsement from the moviegoing public led many industry observers to later look back on this period of time and call it the "golden age" of drive-in movie theaters.

It also became all too obvious to owners that the majority of their patrons weren't flocking past the ticket booth in droves just to view a second-rate film. Rather, owners rightly suspected that it was the "drive-in experience" that kept many moviegoers coming back night after night. *Time* magazine noted, "Despite the fact that producers refuse to sell Drive-Ins anything but old A pictures, punk Bs and westerns, most of them manage to make a respectable profit."[2]

The carnival-like atmosphere that had begun in the mid-1940s reached its high point during the 1950s. Owners, standing on the firm belief that the

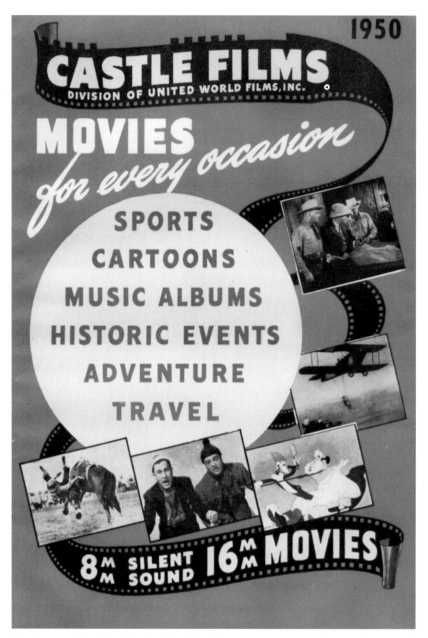

Brochure offered by Castle Films for theater owners. *(Author's collection)*

drive-in craze was taking the country by storm, took full advantage of the opportunity to profit from it as much as possible. To lure in an even higher percentage of the family trade, owners scrambled to devise more innovative and creative ways to draw attention to their theaters.

The Starlite Drive-In in Oak Lawn, Illinois, was well recognized for its wholesome, family atmosphere. One of the larger drive-ins in the area, the Starlite could hold 1,875 automobiles, and it could also accommodate 1,000 walk-in patrons.

To lure in more customers, owners of the Starlite started to give away door prizes to every child under twelve. To everyone else, they handed out the Starlite *Happiness Book.*

The *Happiness Book* contained a number of coupons that were redeemable at either the ticket booth, for the next return trip to the drive-in, or the concession stand. The *Happiness Book* was especially appealing to teenagers who saw it as "extra spending money" to use while out on a date. The owners of the Starlite knew that if their patrons felt like they were getting a bargain with the coupon book they might be enticed to spend more, figuring that they were saving money anyway. "With a *Happiness Book* a youth brings his girl to the Starlite, where we don't sell any alcoholic drinks. We even have attendants in the restrooms to see that nobody spikes the soft drinks. The drive-in is the answer to the problem of wholesome amusement for teenagers."[3]

The focus for the Starlite Drive-In was on good, clean, wholesome fun for the entire family. This idea above all else was a major factor for many owners when choosing the location for their drive-in theater. Parents liked the fact that drive-ins were safe havens for their teenagers.

So, when deciding upon a location to construct a new drive-in, owners were often leery of building next to any establishment that was not seen as family oriented. Drive-ins located near bars, nightclubs, and other drinking facilities could face grave repercussions. In his book, *Drive-In Theater,* George Peterson wrote, "Patrons of those types of entertainment are not the family type of people who are the backbone of the drive-in theater patronage, so no consideration should be given to their possible business."[4]

The Van Nuys Drive-In Theatre (1950) cultivated a "wild west" image. *(Bison Archives)*

Construction of new drive-ins grew at a steady pace during the late 1940s and early 1950s. Owners chose to ignore the fact that too many drive-in movie theaters located in one area of town would cost them business. Drive-in owners in the same vicinity competed with one another to grab the market share of moviegoers. By 1950, the number of drive-ins had risen to over 1,700, as compared to the handful in 1946.[5]

Restrictions were placed on the construction of any new drive-ins in 1952. With a limited supply of building materials available, 600 new drive-ins opened for business. That number was considerably larger than the 65 newly opened indoor houses built that same year. On January 1, 1953, the restrictions were lifted. The National Production Authority estimated that at least 1,000 and possibly as many as 3,000 new drive-ins would be built, bringing the total number to an estimated 4,000.

In 1953, the *New York Times* observed, "Only a few years ago, drive-ins were both scarce and joked about. Even within motion picture circles they were sometimes referred to as 'passion pits' supposedly suitable mainly for convenient parking by amatory twosomes; but if that was ever the case, it certainly is not these days."[6]

The Sunrise Drive-In Theatre had a charming art deco screen.
(Bison Archives)

The construction boom in 1953 prompted some owners to build on a much grander scale than had ever been attempted. The average lot size held an estimated 1,300 cars, but drive-in owners sometimes pushed this to the limit to gain more profits. Owners surmised that since moviegoers didn't necessarily come to see the picture on the screen anyway, it didn't really matter if they were parked so far away that they couldn't see it.

Several drive-in owners advertised their theater as one of the biggest and the best. The All-Weather Drive-In located on Sunrise Highway in Copiague, New York, was one of a handful of large drive-ins. An enormous screen made out of aluminum overlooked a lot that held 2,500 automobiles. The All-Weather also had an indoor theater that could accommodate an additional 1,500 patrons. On a typical night at the All-Weather, "About 100 mothers and children were in the indoor theater watching a double bill, which had started at 5. Outside two boys and two girls rode a small Ferris wheel in a miniature amusement park, and twenty others worked the swings, slides, turntables and a merry-go-round. Ten autos huddled forlornly in the vast lot.

"In fifteen minutes, however, as mealtime approached, autos began to arrive every minute. A miniature four-car train packed with children toured among the autos on the lot.

"By 7 P.M. there were 50 or 60 cars standing there. Almost everyone was eating. By 8 o'clock the great lot was almost full. The small amusement park next to the indoor theater was as jammed as a school playground at recess.

"It was nearly 9 P.M. . . . it was almost time for the outdoor show. Light flooded the great screen and everybody streaked for their cars. By the time the cartoons had materialized, they had all got in, slammed the doors, pulled the electronic speaker inside and settled back for *Johnny Tremain* and *Joe Butterfly*."[7]

Speakers stand at the ready at the Studio Drive-In, Southern California, 1950. *(Bison Archives)*

Other colossal drive-in movie theaters included the 110 Drive-In in Melville, New York, with a lot that held 2,500 cars; the Los Altos Drive-In in Long Beach, California, with a capacity of 2,150 cars; and the Newark Drive-In in Newark, New Jersey, with space available to hold 2,400 automobiles.

At the other end of the spectrum, some owners boasted that their drive-in was the smallest. The Norwood Drive-in in Norwood, Colorado, held 64 cars, while the Highway Drive-In in South Carolina held 50.

Another trend for owners was personalizing their facilities. Many drive-ins were designed around a theme or an idea based on the theater's location or the owner's personal taste. The trick was to

A postcard souvenir from the Circle Drive-In Theatre.
(Robert Giles collection)

lay out the theater and then see what could be added to make it more appealing but at a very small cost to the owner.

The Cedar Valley Drive-In in Rome, Georgia, was designed to replicate a Southern plantation house. The Dixie Summer Gardens Drive-In was an example of a drive-in transformed into a country amusement park. Built in the late 1940s, the 760-car lot on Kentucky's Route 42 was more commonly known as the Gateway to the South.

During a trip to the Dixie Summer Gardens, "Patrons enter the theater along a winding drive. In the center of the entrance area, one's attention is immediately arrested by a large attraction board, which is topped by a massive horseshoe.

"A low red brick wall and painted white fence, which maintains the architectural theme of this famed horse-breeding locality, flank the main entrance area. To the right of the gates stands the red brick box-office. On the roof of the box-office building is a dovecote.

"The administration building is a Southern Colonial mansion of white siding and green shutters and a base of red brick. A pond immediately in front of the building serves both to separate the entrance and exit drives and enhance the setting.

"Centered in the parking area is a building of simplified Colonial design to house the projection booth, confection lobby, and restrooms. Walls of the lobby are glazed of tile.

"The pond in front of the administration building is also used for skating."[8]

Along with the "look" of the drive-in, owners continued to sell an atmosphere based on wholesome family entertainment. Added to the list of amuse-

A friendly Filmack reminder to remove the speaker before driving away. *(Mark Bialek collection)*

Drive-In Theatre Manufacturing
Company, Kansas City, Kansas.
(Robert Giles collection)

ments for some drive-ins were pony rides and full-scale playgrounds with swings, merry-go-rounds, slides, sandboxes, and teeter-totters. Some drive-ins added miniature golf courses and small ponds for boat rides.

The *Motion Picture Herald* observed, "Accentuating the view that the drive-in is a family theater where harried parents can take the youngsters and park them either in—or outside the car—without worry, open air theaters are going in heavily for children's playgrounds, some of them on a very elaborate scale. An empty space near the screen is used as a playground. In areas where summer twilight delays outdoor showings, drive-ins have installed pony rides as an added attraction for the family trade. Some drive-ins offer cut-rate prices for children and may play an hour of children's music before the start of the show."[9]

By 1956, nearly 90 percent of drive-ins had some type of playground facility. It was usually located in the space in front of the screen, but some owners opted to place it closer to the concession stand.

As drive-in owners competed against each other for a larger share of the family trade, their playgrounds became increasingly elaborate. Some owners doubled the size of their playground facility and added newer and more exciting rides. Owners didn't necessarily mind the cost of the expansion because more families meant that their snack bar facilities were doing a thriving business. At a cost averaging $600 or more, many were simply nothing more than a merry-go-round with a swing set inside a sandbox. On a more elaborate scale, some drive-in owners created entire "kiddy lands" for their younger patrons.

The playground at the Hilltop Drive-In contained a twelve-foot-high all-steel slide. Added to this was a castle walk, a merry-go-round, and two sets of swings. Owners opened the playground one hour before show time and assigned two employees to watch the children so that parents could relax and enjoy themselves. Owners quickly noted with satisfaction that the children would often take breaks from playing to go into the concession building and make several small purchases.

A Detroit facility provided two kiddy-land parks. One was free for the movie patrons' children, the other charged a small fee for rides on a perfect-to-scale Wabash Cannonball train. This playground also had its own concession stand.

Postcards promoting *(from top)* Circle Drive-In, Gull Drive-In, Spud Drive-In (in Idaho, naturally), Theatre Motel. *(Robert Giles collection)*

WORLD'S FIRST PRIVATE SCREEN THEATRE - BUFFALO, MO.

Postcard of the Buffalo, Missouri, Drive-In Theatre, which presented an interesting variation on the drive-in formula. *(Robert Giles collection)*

Eventually, swimming pools, miniature zoos, miniature golf, and live bands were utilized at drive-ins in an effort to whet the appetites of hungry moviegoers. Larger drive-ins located in heavily populated areas were adding things like ice skating rinks and full-scale restaurants to their facilities. Some critics complained that drive-ins had gone too far to get the public's attention: "There is every reason to consider the feasibility of other adult amusements than motion pictures. Where will be the first drive-in to have a bowling pavilion?"[10]

The Walter Reade Theaters also had a unique way of attracting new family business. Along with the usual playground, the Reade Drive-In had fireworks exhibits and live animal acts. Free passes were given out to every parent with a newborn baby, up to three months old. The owners hoped that this would remind parents that, unlike at traditional theaters, all members of the family, no matter what age, were welcome at the drive-in, solving the problem of having to hire a babysitter.

The tie-in to many of these enticements was the concession stand. Customers attended the drive-in for all the added amusements, which resulted in much higher profits at the snack bar.

Giveaway contests were also big for attracting higher concession sales. To find out if they had won a prize, patrons were required to make a trip to the snack bar. While waiting to find out if they were indeed the lucky ticket holder, customers often purchased items on impulse.

Spending a night out at the drive-in served as a rite of passage for many young moviegoers. Teenagers loved to take their dates to the drive-in because it afforded them some privacy. Sneaking into the drive-in was another rite of passage. Creative ways of getting past the ticket booth unnoticed included hiding out in the trunk, running alongside the car, or riding on the side-board. Although managers instructed their employees that anyone caught sneaking into the drive-in should be quickly escorted to the exit, this rule was not always strictly enforced. Many owners felt that business was so good that a few patrons sneaking in couldn't possibly hurt overall profits, and those that did sneak in would probably make up for the price of their ticket by buying snacks at the concession stand anyway. Nonetheless, employees were on the lookout for cars that appeared especially heavy in the rear.

A cartoon overlooks the playground equipment at a drive-in in Waco, Texas. *(Robert Giles collection)*

The *New York Times* described the situation this way: "Drive-in admission prices now are per person, as contrasted with the early per-vehicle rate. This ticket standard has resulted in certain special admonitions for drive-in operating staff. Cashiers must train themselves to be ever watchful for unusual circumstances or abnormal behavior on the part of the occupants in any car. They must call the manager's attention to any car which seems to be extraordinarily heavy or 'weighted down' upon its springs. This can indicate patrons hiding in luggage compartments, etc. The action dealing with such cars is the manager's responsibility."[11]

It was obvious that much of the moviegoing public preferred to go to drive-ins rather than indoor movie houses. Film distribution companies found a way to get their share of the profits by changing their film rental policy. Basically, drive-in owners were now required to pay a gross percentage of the film's receipts rather than a standard flat rental fee. Owners were outraged by the change in policy, mainly because even now they were still not getting access to first-run quality films. In protest, many owners gave free admission to all children under the age of twelve and went back to charging a flat per-car rate. Owners were victorious in their battle with the film companies because pricing policies set by drive-in owners could not be regulated by distributors.

But drive-in owners had set their sights even higher. Many longed to become a valued part of their community. Some owners let local churches and civic groups use their lots during the day as a meeting place. In this way, drive-in owners tried to associate themselves with "the pattern of all that is best in everyday living."[12]

Churches preferred holding their services at the drive-in because it allowed all members access to services, from the young family with children to the handicapped and the aged. Owners also believed that they might reap an unexpected benefit from their generosity: once some of these churchgoers saw what the drive-in was like, they might come back in the evening to attend the show.

Sonny obviously tried to cover all his bases and cater to everyone. The drive-in, not mentioned on this postcard, is in the background. *(Robert Giles collection.)*

Studio Drive-In, Southern California, 1950.
(Bison Archives)

The Winter Park Drive-In, located in Orlando, Florida, leased out its lot to the Central Christian Church for its services held every Sunday. The Whitestone Drive-In, in New York, made its facilities available to all faiths. Services were performed by the Protestant Council of the City of New York.

Kerry Seagrave described the services in his book, *Drive-In Theaters: A History From Their Inception in 1933,* "Printed programs of the services were provided to patrons. Each theater had a choir, soloists, and an electric organ. Services were conduced from the top of the projection booths. Patrons listened through the regular in-car speakers. Local firms donated coffee and doughnuts, which were dispensed free from the concession booth before and after the service. Services went ahead rain or shine."[13]

The popularity of drive-ins reached its zenith in 1958, when there were over 4,000 drive-in theaters open for business. Owners continued to be pleased with the large profits they pulled in nightly. The "car culture" that continued in America was fast becoming a commodity for drive-in movie theaters. People were buying cars faster than Detroit could produce them. An estimated 50 million automobiles traveled America's roadways. Freeways were being built to make driving safer, and people were spending more time in their cars.

The *New York Times Magazine* pointed out in 1955 that the drive-in, "once scorned as odd, even disreputable—the movies were always very old and very bad, the audiences not always solely interested in the movies—has become solid and respectable. Today it is, in fact, big business. From the insignificant 300 in 1946, drive-ins have multiplied startlingly to the present 4,062. They attract millions of car-borne families, and serve the community somewhat as a social center. While drive-ins have boomed in the last decade, regular movie houses have dropped in number."[14]

During the mid- to late-1950s drive-ins began premiering "horror" and "sci-fi adventure" weekend theme nights. As they continued to battle the

To gain respect in the community, some owners donated their theaters to church congregations to hold Sunday services. The churches were happy to have the space because it allowed many more people to attend than might otherwise. *(Robert Giles collection)*

studios for better quality films, they tried to make the best of what they had. The tie-in to many of these ideas was, again, the concession stand. Owners would create an atmosphere that paralleled the movies on the screen. Rather than sit in their cars and watch a second-rate film, moviegoers would hang out at the snack bar. The concession stand became the focal point at the drive-in, a place where customers would congregate to socialize with friends and neighbors.

When television was introduced into the American household in the 1950s, movie attendance declined in general. But while many indoor theaters reported a decline in business, drive-ins continued to do a steady business. In fact, they were credited with keeping Hollywood afloat during this transition period.

However, by the late 1950s the public's perception of drive-in movie theaters slowly began to change. Sound quality was still a major problem for outdoor theaters. Many indoor movie houses were now beginning to feature CinemaScope, a system that produced stereo sound. They were trying to make the moviegoing experience vastly different from watching the tiny black and white screen of the increasingly popular television.

Advertisement from *Boxoffice* magazine. *(Author's collection)*

The few drive-ins that tried to implement CinemaScope failed miserably. However, most owners didn't worry about installing the new sound system, due in part to the fact that they were still making plenty of money with the old system. Since the public was still coming out to the drive-in, owners felt confident that drive-in movie theaters would continue to do a thriving business, despite their inferior technological offerings. However, according to Kerry Seagrave, "the drive-in was growing both in number and size faster than the public cared to visit it. While the numbers indicated this by 1958 nobody in the industry seemed to notice. There was no warning of overbuilding or of a stagnant or lagging audience."[15]

The frenzy that surrounded drive-ins for so long had finally begun to slow down considerably, along with the public's perception of them. By the end of the 1950s and well into the 1960s, drive-in movie theater owners

were forced to face the sad and harsh reality that their "golden decade" was coming to an end. By the middle of the next decade it would become obvious to many industry insiders that drive-in movie theaters were in real trouble.

Drive-ins offered their patrons in-car heaters that hung on the speaker poles, allowing the drive-in experience to last year round. *(Author's collection)*

In 1957, at the height of the drive-in craze, the world premiere of *The Devil's Hairpin* was held at the Victory Drive-In Theatre. *(Bison Archives)*

Advertisement for Bengies Drive-In Theater. *(Terry Lee Roth collection)*

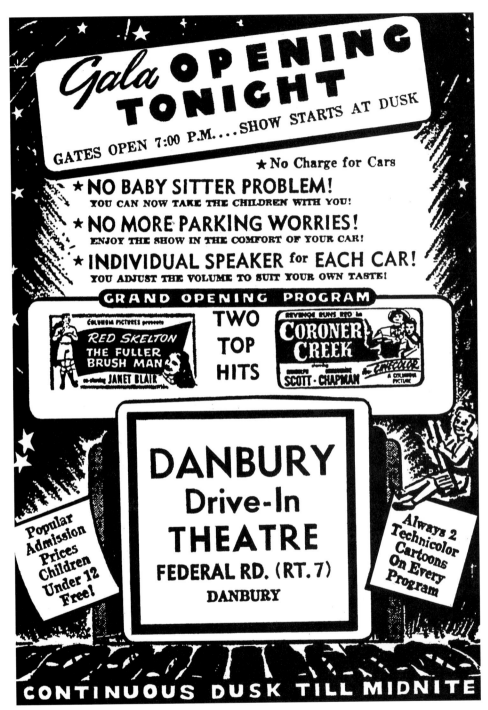

Advertisement for the Danbury Drive-In Theatre. *(Mark Bialek collection)*

The Victory Drive-In, another theater with an elaborately decorated screen. *(Bison Archives)*

The influence of the early 1960s is evident in the design of the Gilmore Drive-In
Theater, 1960. *(Bison Archives)*

309 Drive-In Theatre marquee; note the "in-car heaters" that allowed the theater to stay open all winter. *(Bison Archives)*

The Woodbridge Drive-In Theatre is showing a combination of scary and family films—appealing to both teens and parents with small children. *(Bison Archives)*

The frenzied and sometimes manic atmosphere that had surrounded so many drive-in movie theaters during the mid- to late-1950s was already beginning to die out by the early 1960s.

While a large portion of the moviegoing public still opted to enjoy a night out under the stars, their numbers were nowhere near those recorded just a few years earlier. Many industry insiders began to suspect that this overall decline in audience attendance was a sure sign of the beginning of the end for the drive-in movie theater.

Drive-in owners who had failed to modernize their facilities now found themselves struggling to stay open for business. By the mid-1960s, drive-in movie theaters were losing business at a startling rate.

During the 1940s and 1950s drive-ins had appealed to families with children. And because of the baby boom, this segment of the population made up a large percentage of audience membership. By the mid-1960s, the population distribution had changed. As times changed, so did the family unit. Owners became aware of the changes in their audience, which was now made up of a smaller portion of families. The majority of drive-in moviegoers were now teenagers and young couples.

The voracious media coverage that had once surrounded open-air theaters had also slowed considerably, since there was little if anything new to report. The industry remained stagnant, refusing to advance technologically as indoor theaters had done.

Owners who had at one time run successful and profitable operations couldn't help but be concerned over the changing atmosphere of their industry. Many were reluctant to accept the fact that the "drive-in experience" with all its amenities was no longer luring the crowds of the previous decade.

The *Motion Picture Herald* cautioned, "At the time when the drive-in was still an incidental operation of no particular importance to the distributors, the outdoor theaters were content in playing old pictures, not caring much what was shown on their screens. They usually received last runs, paying flat rentals, and seldom were there any difficulties with neighboring exhibitors. Today the situation is causing concern."[1]

Drive-In theater, Los Angeles, California. *(Bison Archives)*

By the mid-1960s it appeared that the novelty of going to the drive-in was definitely wearing off. The carnival atmosphere that had worked so well for many owners was no longer effective. A large number of drive-in patrons were simply no longer willing to pay to see second-run features heard through a poor sound system. Instead, they patronized their local indoor theater.

Owners were woefully unprepared for this shift in the public's taste from wholesome outdoor fun to quality cinema. Many owners now paid a high price for never having bothered to upgrade their facility or gain access to better quality films.

All the evidence pointed to an industry in serious trouble. Owners now faced the question of how to quickly gain back their audience share. Between television and newly renovated indoor theaters, the competition was stiff, and owners knew that they had to come up with original and innovative ideas that would steer the audience back to the drive-in.

One such innovation came about in 1963. The owners of the Autoscope Drive-In, located in Albuquerque, New Mexico, opted to structurally change their drive-in movie theater so that it was tailor made for each audience member, or at least each carload. Instead of projecting the movie onto a large flat screen in the normal way, the owners of the Autoscope installed 260 small screens, one in front of each vehicle. A number of mirrors were then installed to reflect the movie from one central projector.

The owners of the Autoscope believed that showing such personal attention to each moviegoer would help make their patrons feel more at home while watching the film. Although the Autoscope system was new and innovative, the idea never caught on.

The Theatre Motel, located in Battlesboro, Vermont, was another new innovation. Serving as a regular drive-in theater with a lot that could accommodate several hundred automobiles, the motel also had rooms that faced the 100-foot screen. Anyone interested in watching the movie had the option of paying the regular admission fee of seventy-five cents to watch

A line of cars waits to get into the Greater Pittsburgh Five Drive-In Theaters, North Versailles, Pennsylvania. *(Terry Lee Roth collection)*

Haar's Drive-In, Dillsburg, Pennsylvania. *(Debrean and Randy Loy collection)*

the film from their car or pay a minimum of sixteen dollars and get a room at the motel, which was equipped with speakers. Besides all the usual amenities, guests of the motel could enjoy seeing the movie from the privacy of their own room. The air-conditioned rooms were often preferable to a car, especially in the hot summer months. Although the Theatre Motel was successful, it remained one of a kind, never serving as a blueprint for other would-be motel drive-ins.

As hard as they tried, many owners failed to come up with new ways of recapturing the golden era of the 1950s. They came to face the harsh reality that those halcyon days were now a part of history.

Looking for any way to generate profits and move a steady stream of customers through their ticket booths, many owners desperately resorted to showing R-rated and soft-core pornographic films, which created a whole new set of problems. Until now, drive-ins had been widely regarded as a wholesome place for family entertainment, although their reputation as a make-out location for teenagers was well known. Fundamentalist groups from around the country were up in arms that such films were being featured in their neighborhoods. They claimed that not only could children see the offensive material, it was a distraction to drivers on the highway.

As these groups sought legal remedies to stop owners from showing the adult films, some courts ruled that drive-ins could continue in the practice, since many indoor houses were showing the same material. Others levied fines against drive-in owners who showed adult films.

It seemed that drive-ins and their owners were again caught in the middle of a swirling controversy. Like previous issues they had dealt with, this one also eventually reached the Supreme Court. The high court ruled that states could *not* invoke fines against owners for showing adult films.

But many states found clever ways to get around the ruling, such as citing owners with obscenity laws if the images could be seen by the public from outside the property lines of the theater.

One drive-in owner in North Carolina who wanted to comply with all laws applied for a permit to build a nine-foot fence around his drive-

Concession stand at the Rodeo Triplex Drive-In, Port Orchard, Washington. *(Ken Layton collection)*

in. Such a fence would ensure that the public would not be able to catch a glimpse of the movie. Ironically, local zoning boards denied his request to erect the fence, stating that fences were limited to a height of three feet.

The owner of the Orange Drive-In faced another dilemma when he decided to expand his operation by adding a second screen. His theater was located between two townships. The first screen was located in Orange, California, and the other in Anaheim. Officials in Orange had no problem with the owner showing any kind of movie he wanted, but those in Anaheim placed a limit on what could be shown, claiming that they wanted to maintain their reputation for wholesome family fun, especially with Disneyland located close by.

One South Carolina drive-in owner attempted to please everyone by switching back and forth between playing religious films and soft porn: "The Pentecostals will line up for Pat Boone's *The Cross and the Switchblade* and anything with an Art Linkletter voice-over. But then there's a lot of folks down here who would just soon see what Linda Lovelace is doing too. You want to know the best drive-in movie ever made? *Thunder Road.* Don't ask me why. Maybe it's the chases, maybe it's Robert Mitchum. But it's a door-buster. I could bring it in tomorrow and I'd be packed."[2]

Ticket booth at the Mission Drive-In, Pomona, California.
(Michael McKeon collection)

Many owners, no longer willing to try to get their audience back or not wanting to pay for upgrades to their facility, opted to get out of the business altogether. They sold off their land to the highest bidder to minimize further losses.

If owners had only waited a few more years to sell they may have gotten considerably more money for their land, since land values sky-rocketed in the 1970s. Instead, many panicked and settled for what was offered to them just to get out of the business, which they were increasingly coming to view as a sinkhole. The *Los Angeles Times* observed, "The sprawling complexes fell victim to changing tastes and rising land values. Housing tracts, shopping malls and self-storage facilities now sit on lots where science-fiction flicks and other films played before budding baby boomers."[3]

Indeed, throughout the 1960s, drive-in theaters became more and more scarce, and the trend continued during the next two decades. Drive-in movie theaters were fading from the American landscape by the time the mid-1970s and 1980s rolled around. Across the country, hundreds of drive-in movie theaters, which had once brightly lined the nation's highways with their flashing neon lights and billowing screen towers, were now closed. Their vacant lots became magnets for vandalism and overgrown weeds.

Chester Liebs in *Main Street to Miracle Mile* wrote, "Where once hundreds of cars could be seen by night, eerily encircled about a glowing image, there are now office buildings, condominiums, and shopping malls. In areas where patronage has declined and land values have not risen, many drive-ins have simply been abandoned, leaving the ghostly hulk of a screen tower as a symbol of mid-twentieth-century America's passion for the automobile."[4]

Drive-in movie theaters had exploded onto the landscape in the early part of the 1950s, due in part to relatively inexpensive and available land. As more people opted to move away from overcrowded cities to the suburbs, the drive-ins had followed suit. The car culture that swept across America also had a hand in promoting the industry. Gasoline was cheap and Americans loved to drive anywhere in their large, comfortable automobiles.

Thirty years later, many key factors that had helped make the drive-in movie theater a phenomenal success would play major roles in its demise. The development of any new drive-in movie theater during the late 1970s was highly impractical.

Mission Drive-In, Pomona, California: *(top)* concession stand; *(bottom)* marquee. *(Michael McKeon collection)*

Auto-Vue Theatre, Colville, Washington. *(Robert Everett collection)*

They were not the cash cows they had once been and were considered extremely risky.

Land values and overriding costs deterred many investors from making a commitment to a new drive-in. The high cost of real estate made it nearly impossible for a developer to build a new drive-in movie theater since it would require a lot ranging anywhere from ten to twenty acres in size.

The drive-in owners that were still trying to survive realized that to sustain audience attendance something had to be done immediately to help the sagging industry. Many owners agreed that technological improvements were mandatory to fuel new growth. Smaller changes had occurred, but they didn't necessarily create headline news, which the struggling theaters needed.

Some drive-ins introduced the curved CinemaScope screens, producing sharper images. Also, most owners began broadcasting the movie's soundtrack over AM radio stations, eliminating the tinny, antiquated speakers.[5] This small improvement helped in sound quality but didn't greatly affect audience attendance.

Unwilling to accept that drive-in movie theaters were destined to be a part of the past and not the future, one company, which already owned a chain of drive-ins, made the bold announcement that they were proceeding with plans to build a newer, more futuristic type of drive-in movie theater. Pacific Theaters Corporation in California announced that their company would be erecting two new drive-in movie theaters in the Southern California area. The focus for these new theaters was that they would be tailor made for moviegoers. Both theaters would have a car capacity of up to 5,000 vehicles. Spaces would be customized to fit any type of car, be it a van or a compact model. The installation of an electric conveyor walkway would aid patrons on their way to the concession building. Other features were to include a daylight screen and self maintaining restrooms. The design of the lot was to resemble a country park. Sadly, but not surprisingly, these drive-ins never made it past the blueprint stage.

Most owners, rather than looking toward the future of drive-ins, were looking for a way to get *out* of the doomed industry. When the cost of real estate began to climb, those owners who had weathered the decline and held onto their theaters realized that they were sitting on virtual gold mines. Land that had cost $100,000 three decades ago was now fetching up to a million dollars or more, depending upon the lot size and location. Suddenly, "A drive-in was a business you went into to make a living, while real estate values went up."[6]

The temptation to sell to real estate agents was great since many drive-ins were no longer turning a profit. But until an offer was put on the table, many owners had to resort to other tactics to try and carve out a living. Some owners leased out their lots on weekends for swap meets, flea markets, or classic car clubs.

Drive-ins that were chosen for the

This screen tower at the Rodeo Triplex Drive-In, Port Orchard, Washington, doesn't exhibit any of the enticing paintings or art deco designs of yesteryear. *(Ken Layton collection)*

wrecking ball were often located near major thoroughfares, where access to new buildings made buying up the facility all the more appealing. As drive-ins faded from the landscape they were quickly replaced with now-familiar American sights: shopping malls, office buildings, hotels, restaurants, and new housing developments. *Boxoffice* magazine observed in 1984, "Existing drive-in operators are finding that either out-right sale of their land or its development for shopping malls or industrial locations provide attractive incentives to get out of the exhibition business."[7]

The car culture, which had been a huge influence on the popularity of the drive-in, subsided due to a number of factors. In the 1970s, the gas embargo resulted in a sharp decline in pleasure driving. Customers that had to wait in long lines at the gas pump were going to be much more conservative about their chosen destination. This resulted in a drastic decrease in audience attendance at drive-in movie theaters.

The sign at the Sunset Drive-In in Tumwater, Washington, shows a little wear and tear. *(Ken Layton collection)*

Automobile design was another element that played a role in the drive-in's decline. Newer, foreign models rolling off assembly lines were smaller and not as comfortable as cars made back in the 1950s. It was uncomfortable to sit in small bucket seats for the duration of two feature films, a cartoon and sometimes a newsreel. Inga Saffron, writing in the *Philadelphia Inquirer*, noted, "Americans had viewed their cars as second living rooms. By the 1980s, the country, still smarting from the gas crisis, thought of the automobile as more like a bathroom, a necessity."[8]

Why should Americans sit in their cars to watch movies when at home they had their La-Z-Boy recliners? Complete home entertainment systems were fast becoming the latest craze. Just as television had once threatened the movie industry in the 1950s, the newest predator was *cable* television. With the advent of large screen TVs and VCRs, Americans had literally transformed their living rooms into home theaters. Another added bonus was that unlike at the drive-in, the concession stand at home was a short, indoor walk away—the kitchen.

Audiences had also changed considerably by the 1970s and 1980s. At the peak of their popularity, drive-ins had catered to families with young children.

This demographic had attended the drive-in, on average, four times a month. No longer was that true. Individuals or couples were now the main attendees for drive-ins, and they allotted time to see a movie, on average, about twice a month.

Back in the 1950s, teenagers went to the drive-in to hang out with their peers. But now shopping malls were fast becoming the preferred spot to gather and mingle. Many indoor theaters, trying to capitalize on this trend, attached themselves to these prime locations with great results.

The words on this marquee are common at drive-ins in colder climates. *(Ken Layton collection)*

With many factors at play in the decline of the drive-in movie theater, some owners simply stopped offering added amenities. Long gone was the carnival-like atmosphere that had once lured crowds to the drive-in on a Saturday night. Playgrounds that had once entertained swarms of children were now a thing of the past, as were the children that played on them. Due to the high cost of insurance premiums, a majority of owners opted to tear down and dismantle their playgrounds, train tracks, and dance floors for fear of lawsuits.

The decade of the 1970s also saw a change in the design for indoor movie houses. Single screen facilities were becoming multiplexes. By dividing a theater into several screens, indoor theater owners were able to increase attendance. Drive-ins, on the other hand, did not easily lend themselves to the multiplex design. Although as many as 10 percent of the remaining drive-ins did convert, it was a complicated process. The placement of the screen had to be taken into consideration so that it was not in direct sunlight. If this happened it would further delay showing the feature film during the summer months when daylight savings time was in effect.

Another reason many drive-in owners declined to multiplex their facility was the cost. Many drive-in facilities would first require a general overhaul before multiplexing could even be considered. Because owners had failed to maintain their facilities while business was good, many felt that the cost to upgrade now just wasn't worth the potential reward. They quickly dismissed the idea of changing the look of their drive-in facility if they couldn't foresee any profits to be made by increasing the number of screens. Screen towers

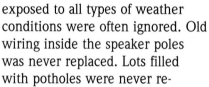

Contemporary examples of drive-in publicity items. *above:* complimentary pass and car club card for the Galaxy Drive-In in North Vandergrift, Pennsylvania *(Jim Lipuma collection);* matchbook for Skyline Drive-in in Shelton, Washington. *(Ken Layton collection)*

exposed to all types of weather conditions were often ignored. Old wiring inside the speaker poles was never replaced. Lots filled with potholes were never re-paved. Sound quality was second rate, and the equipment was never updated.

As in years past, owners continued to battle with production companies over the showing of first-run films. Certain production companies were out-fitted to make films exclusively for drive-ins. These genre films were a double threat: low budget and low quality. Science fiction, slasher, or action movies produced by these companies were often the only thing that kept a drive-in owner in business. The quality of the film was certainly not the draw, but the subject matter appealed to a specific audience.

And so it came as a blow to drive-in owners when many of these production companies bowed out of the drive-in business, opting to take their films directly to cable television. Owners had no choice but to make do with what was available to them. And even today some owners still hold to the old belief that it is the drive-in experience and not the film that really matters.

Although the number of drive-in movie theaters is dwindling, those that are still in operation seem to be able to keep a steady business of regular customers, who are drawn to the nostalgia factor and the low price. Indeed, according to the *Los Angeles Times,* "Some

drive-in owners say the industry's long decline may have ended."⁹

And there's another sign that drive-ins aren't gone for good. A small but dedicated group of people who value drive-in movie theaters have bought and reopened theaters that were once closed and abandoned. Two budding entrepreneurs, Fred Baum and Greg Reinhold, have purchased the Hamilton Drive-In. They restored and renovated the facility by adding new neon to its exterior along with an updated snack bar and box office. Thousands of dollars also went toward improving the sound quality. Baum, a former employee of the Holiday Drive-In, obviously saw potential in keeping the Hamilton up and running. Others across the country have followed suit.

above and below: Capitol Drive-In, San Jose, California. *(Anne Dominion collection)*

The Suburban Drive-In in Gainesville, Florida, is an abandoned and run-down theater that was rescued by current owners Pete Hudnall and Phil Gibson, who bought the drive-in and gave it a much needed face-lift. Hudnall and Gibson decided to multiplex the Suburban. Because it is located in a college town, the Suburban features films aimed at a younger crowd.

The *Los Angeles Times* highlighted an interesting factor about the recent surge in drive-in attendance: "Those drive-ins that have successfully bucked the trend have mimicked walk-in theaters by replacing single screens with four, six and even eight screens. Low budget, second-run action films have

It takes all of this intimidating equipment to run a film at the Rodeo Triplex in Port Orchard, Washington. *(Ken Layton collection)*

been replaced by first-run features that often appeal to young families."[10] And so it appears that the drive-in has come full circle—it is again a place for parents to bring the kids and enjoy an evening out with the family.

The drive-in serves as a proud reminder of what can result from one man's idea. It was the vision of Richard Hollingshead Jr. over half a century ago that brought forth this uniquely American cultural and historical icon. Today there are fewer than 800 drive-ins open for business. They provide a link to our past and will always be a part of our American landscape. They're still out there, neon lights, concession stands, speakers, and all, waiting to share with a new generation the thrill of watching a movie under the stars.

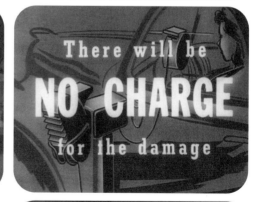

Debrean and Randy Loy, who were kind enough to provide some of the photos in this book, publish a guidebook to operational drive-ins. It's an excellent resource.

Notes

Introduction

†   Chester H. Liebs. *Main Street to Miracle Mile, American Roadside Architecture.* Boston: A New York Graphic Society Book/Little, Brown and Company. 1985.

Sneak Preview

1. Richard M. Hollingshead, Jr. "Drive-In Theater." U.S. Patent Office. May 16, 1933. Patent number 1,909,537.
2. Floyd E. Stone. "Father of Drive-Ins Says 'Never Again.'" *Motion Picture Herald.* January 28, 1950.
3. Richard M. Hollingshead, Jr. "Drive-In Theater." U.S. Patent Office. May 16, 1933. Patent number 1,909,537.
4. "Drive-In Theater to Be Opened Here." *Courier-Post.* May 17, 1933.
5. Brad Angier. "New England Open-Air Theater Situation Forsakes Ozone for Courtroom Battles." *Boxoffice.* April 30, 1938.
6. "Loew's Drive-In Theaters Inc. *v.* Park-In Theaters, Inc." *United States Patent Quarterly.* 81:149-55.
7. Floyd E. Stone. "Father of Drive-Ins Says 'Never Again.'" *Motion Picture Herald.* January 28, 1950.
8. "Drive-In Theater." *Collier's.* March 22, 1938.
9. "Spread of Drive-In Cinemas May Become a Worry to Regular Ops; Dixie Belt Can Stay Open All Year." *Variety.* July 6, 1938.

Shankweiler's

1. Dale Schneck. "America's Oldest Drive-In Theater." *Boxoffice.* September 1983.
2. Ibid.

Ticket to Paradise

1. Thomas M. Pryor. "Movie Novelty Develops Into Big Business." *New York Times.* September 4, 1949.
2. Ibid.

3. "The Roof's the Sky and the Sky Is Drive-In Limit." *Motion Picture Herald.* July 17, 1948.
4. "389 New Theaters Entered Field in 1939." *Boxoffice.* February 10, 1940.
5. Fred Hift. "Drive-Ins a'Bloom in Springs—By Hundreds." *Motion Picture Herald.* March 26, 1949.
6. Ibid.
7. Thomas M. Pryor. "Movie Novelty Develops Into Big Business." *New York Times.* September 4, 1949.
8. Fred Hift. "Drive-Ins a'Bloom in Springs—By Hundreds." *Motion Picture Herald.* March 26, 1949.
9. "The Roof's the Sky and the Sky Is Drive-In Limit." *Motion Picture Herald.* July 17, 1948.
10. Fred Hift. "Drive-Ins a'Bloom in Springs—By Hundreds." *Motion Picture Herald.* March 26, 1949.
11. Ibid.
12. "Cinema." *Time.* June 20, 1949.
13. Chester H. Liebs. *Main Street to Miracle Mile, American Roadside Architecture.* Boston: A New York Graphic Society Book/Little, Brown and Company. 1985.
14. "The Roof's the Sky and the Sky Is Drive-In Limit." *Motion Picture Herald.* July 17, 1948.
15. Kerry Seagrave. *Drive-In Theaters: A History From Their Inception in 1933.* Jefferson, North Carolina, and London: McFarland & Company, Inc., Publishers. 1992.
16. Thomas M. Pryor. "Movie Novelty Develops Into Big Business." *New York Times.* September 4, 1949.
17. Ibid.

At the Snack Bar

1. Kerry Seagrave. *Drive-In Theaters: A History From Their Inception in 1933.* Jefferson, North Carolina, and London: McFarland & Company, Inc., Publishers. 1992.
2. Ansel M. Moore. "The Drive-In Theory:

Basically Sound But Badly Interpreted." *Boxoffice.* December 8, 1945.

3. Thomas M. Pryor. "Movie Novelty Develops Into Big Business." *New York Times.* September 4, 1949.

4. "The Roof's the Sky and Sky Is Drive-In Limit." *Motion Picture Herald.* July 17, 1948.

5. "Drive-In Owners Want Per Person Admission, Earlier Product Run." *Motion Picture Herald.* June 30, 1951.

6. Kerry Seagrave. *Drive-In Theaters, A History From Their Inception in 1933.* Jefferson, North Carolina, and London: McFarland & Company, Inc., Publishers. 1992.

7. Fred Hift. "Drive-Ins a'Bloom in Springs—By Hundreds." *Motion Picture Herald.* March 26, 1949.

8. Wilfred P. Smith. "Is Your Refresheteria Ready for 1951?" *Motion Picture Herald.* January 6, 1951.

9. Frances Harding. "Cafeteria Service Spells CASH at the Drive-In." *Boxoffice.* July 7, 1951.

10. Ibid.

Double Feature

1. Thomas M. Pryor. "Movie Novelty Develops Into Big Business." *New York Times.* September 4, 1949.

2. "Drive-Ins." *Time.* July 14, 1941.

3. Frank J. Taylor. "Big Boom in Outdoor Movies." *Saturday Evening Post.* September 15, 1956.

4. George M. Peterson. *Drive-In Theater.* Kansas City, Missouri: Associated Publication. 1953.

5. "Drive-In Theaters of the 1950 Season." *Theater Catalog.* 1949–1950.

6. Leonard Spinrad. "Burgeoning Drive-Ins: Building Boom in Open Air Houses Expected." *New York Times.* March 1, 1953.

7. "The Colossal Drive-In." *Newsweek.* July 22, 1957.

8. "Adapting a Drive-In to Its Countryside." *Better Theaters.* October 1, 1949.

9. "The Roof's the Sky and Sky Is Drive-In Limit." *Motion Picture Herald.* July 17, 1948.

10. "He'd Have Drive-Ins Offer More Than

Movies." *Motion Picture Herald.* November 5, 1949.

11. Leonard Spinrad. "Burgeoning Drive-Ins: Building Boom in Open Air Houses Expected." *New York Times.* March 1, 1953.

12. Ibid.

13. Kerry Seagrave. *Drive-In Theaters, A History From Their Inception in 1933.* Jefferson, North Carolina, and London: McFarland & Company, Inc., Publishers. 1992.

14. "The Family Drives In." *New York Times Magazine.* June 26, 1955.

15. Kerry Seagrave. *Drive-In Theaters, A History From Their Inception in 1933.* Jefferson, North Carolina, and London: McFarland & Company, Inc., Publishers. 1992.

After Dusk

1. "The Roof's the Sky and Sky Is Drive-In Limit." *Motion Picture Herald.* July 17, 1948.

2. Kerry Seagrave. *Drive-In Theaters, A History From Their Inception in 1933.* Jefferson, North Carolina, and London: McFarland & Company, Inc., Publishers. 1992.

3. Jesus Sanchez. "Scene Change." *Los Angeles Times.* August 7, 1989.

4. Chester H. Liebs. *Main Street to Miracle Mile, American Roadside Architecture.* Boston: A New York Graphic Society Book/Little, Brown and Company. 1985.

5. Inga Saffron. "The Last (Drive-In) Picture Show." *Philadelphia Inquirer.* September 30, 1990.

6. Betsy Brown. "Whatever Happened to the Drive-In Movies?" *New York Times.* February 1, 1987.

7. Bruce A. Austin. "Portrait of a Contemporary Drive-In Theater Audience." *Boxoffice.* May 5, 1984.

8. Inga Saffron. "The Last (Drive-In) Picture Show." *Philadelphia Inquirer.* September 30, 1990.

9. Jesus Sanchez. "Scene Change." *Los Angeles Times.* August 7, 1989.

10. Ibid.

Index